Bare Poetry.

(Jazz Poetry & Songs.)

by
M.K. Eugene S. Lange

"The original Urban Griot, hailed by Roger Hill on Radio Merseyside's Popular Music Show, as "The man who brought Black, and Rastafarian art out of Liverpool 8, and woke the City up to it's history of slavery, and exploitation". His grass roots work opened the way for the Trans-Atlantic Slavery Museum, and a host of forward-looking young creatives from Toxteth to emerge."

Phil Calland.

Music Documentary maker, and film producer.

Contents.

92. Lava.
93. Activated.
94. Recognition Ignition.
95. Love's Witness Testifies.
96. Maritime Pines.
97. Masaala.
98. Modern Life.
99. Oral Poesie.
100. Academia.
101. Moments.
102. Morning Song.
103. Mother of Pearl.
104. "One Love!"
105. Sibilance.
106. Biti Benafi.
107. Path.
108. The Crystal Waters.
109. The Pearl.
111. Judgement Blues.
112. Pirate Cove.
113. Wild Frontier Blues.
114. Poetry Blues.
115. Puma.
116. Poirot.
117. Pupation.
118. Serenity.
119. Silent Light.
120. Silence.
121. Soul Shine.
122. Spark.
123. Storm.

Rialto.

Saturday mornings watching Captain Video
fighting in the ailes
leaping from imaginary horses
taking imaginary spaceship rides.

A kid fires an imaginary ray-gun.
Imagines the usherette is a Martian and hides.

Tempting stills from current films
displayed in slim glass cases
in technicolour on the pillars outside
a celluloid circus/creates curiosity on eager faces.

This temple of dreams was the place where Mom
met Pop
a place where the barriers would drop.

Pop was a Black G.I. / An RAF Sealand guy.
Mom was a White Jazz singer with a Blues eye.

Big bands played and people romanced
to the songs of Billy Holliday and Nina Simone.
The Riao' was Kool/ Mom sang the place swang...

In pubs and bars clubs and cars
houses flats and tenement yards
the vibes would flow the music would play
and everybody danced and laughed and played.
The South End swayed
That was back in the day...

Years later the cinema became Swainy's

a store house for second-hand furniture
Social security interior decor for us the poor
where around the corner little blue disabled cars
lined up outside the Robert Jones where people
made red poppies
for Remembrance Day.

This in turn evolved / grew/ developed into
The Rialto Community Centre
where we brought the rhythms of Afrika closer / to
home
as Delado Drum'n'Dance
set a heartical-rootical-crucial tone.
Beat City L8 to the bone

In the territorial rituals of representation
that take place in this globally aware time
and space / the Riao' marked out a peoples
identity...
Cosmopolitan / but nothing fancy
a landmark that sadly lit up the sky one dark
Summer's night.
A piece of history that died / Why ?
Cos the people were forced into a furious fight /
You see authorities very seldom see the light / till
it's much too late
And then the Riao' became an empty space
a reflection of a people's past / A people's face.
A line / a curve / a wave / a trace.......

Time and Spice.

(A piece of Surrealist prose 1991).

But then there was that time… then there was that
time
We were on our way back from Edinburgh man
And yuh know yuh gotta stop over at Glasgow
when your coming from Edinburgh
On your way to the pool
So we stop.
We realise we got a four and a half hour wait
Hanging at the coach terminal
Me and the Cosmic Kid
The Bastard son of Brendan Behan.

We'd been up all night man
And man we we're just spaced out…
Yuh know when your strung out/
When you've been up all night drinking and its
starting to wear off
And we're standing there kinda WIRED…….

And this woman collapses about eight feet in front
of us
Directly in Front of us
I mean …We were looking at her and she just
collapsed there and then
On the very spot
Right in front of our very eyes.

The paramedics turned up looking like mechanics
In green boiler suits & black monkey boots

Looking like mechanics and having about as much luck
Without their antiseptic pick-up truck..... They were sadly and solemnly unstuck.

They're books were of no use.
A carbon based organism.
A Human Being.
A Person had just died right before our very eyes
The song in my mind changed to a kinda Bluesy type of mode
And I realised I had come full circle
And....... I mean.... Everything was different now
But it was kinda strange in the way that it was sorta the same
Zen ? Like hey ! As Kwai Chang Kane would say: 'Who can Say ? "

But there was a difference...Yeah !
Paranoia triggered by insecurity
Yuh know all that kinda loose shit that comes down on yuh when somthun like that happens just outa the blue
But I realised that no matter how much it rained on me
It could nevva really undermine my Faith
Not ever again
Not now...
I was in too much of a Kamikaze-type of a headspace.

I mean ...Even as I write this ...

I'm standing there bathed in the
exhausted indifference that emanates Bliss...
The surrogate son of Brendan Behan
born again as fellow founding member of
The Delftware Poets Society.......
(Enter the Cosmic Kid...)
Stands next to me Silent Agog...
Gob-smacked at lifes ability to
just pop a mind-fuck on a dude.......
When he least expected it.

The lad who coined the phrase "Putting the pottery
back into poetry"
After waking up hung over on Guiness...and Yeah !
Hungover and in Love or was it just lust with a red
haired lassie
After a vain-glorious night of success at the
Edinburgh Fringe Club...

An exstacy that even for me added yet another
Lipgloss-smeared-glimmer-of-shimmering-hope
To one of Life's Golden moments.

Her name was Lorinda
Her father was a G.I.based just outside Edinburgh
Hence the mad name/ Yuh know worra mean ....
"Half Lora-Half Linda"...she explained
Her mother had married someone else...
She was the bastard child of a G.I.
Like Hey ! Who wasn't !...
And anyway she was beautiful
Even if she was on the stocky side

Big boned shall we say.

Lorinda and her actress friend who fancied herself
As Mary Queen of Scots took me and the Cosmic
kid to this late night converted warehouse / kind
of a restaurant / bistro-discobar-sort of place....

Atmospherically ...it was a bit like Eric's Club in
Liverpool used to be
Like in the late 70's to early 80's / Very Punky but
with kind of a 90's Rap thing on top / Kind of a
flat-topped-Hip-hop-or was it a retro Be-bop/ Call
it bip-bop on the way out.......

Or so I thought at the time.

Didn't we meet my step-daughter's long-lost
biological father in there.......
I mean....He musta been the only Black guy in there
apart from yours truly
And as is usually the way the Dames
unsuspectingly thought it was only natural that
I'd know him
I mean you go up to Edinburgh, and there might be
one Black guy in the whole area for miles and the
locals take you to see him.
As if your gonna know him...
And by some strange coincidence you do know
him.
But they're like "There you go we knew you'd know
him... It's only natural like innit !" Like we all know
each other...Right !

I mean....We do in a lateral, abstracted sort of way
But not how they thought.
Except that this time of course it was how they thought...
And by now the only Bajun I know with a Scottish accent was telling me about this group of Black Scots who travel from the Caribbean every year complete with kilts, sporans, dirks, and everything for a kind of 'Roots' type of reunion thang.......

I mean ...Like far-out man !
I mean ...Like really jumping off !
I mean ...What can I say ?

He told me that the Douglas Clan had been started by an African back in 1770...
And he claimed that the bagpipes had originated in Africa.

I said that I did'nt care if it was a Black man or a Whiteman invented the bagpipes Whoever it was needed a damn good sorting out...
He looked offended
I added "Only joking of course some of my best friends play the bag-pipes
He didn't buy it ... But he let it ride.
The funny thing was I was actually telling the truth.

Fate was bowling googlies...And it wasn't over yet...There was some playful under-handers to be delivered before we got back to the Pool.. .And the fun....Hey ! ...Well it wasn't over / not by a long-chalk....Whatever that means.......

Little did we know that 'He who knows who we were
Before we were who we are'...
Would add a tragic-magic to our total acceptance of the awesome beauty of.......
'simply being'.

Did you like that 'simply' ...Well nothing ever happens that simply does it ?...
Not when you look into it with an open mind and an honest heart...
Being ?
Yeah !
We were very much being
Surrendering to Life's unpredictable mysteries
A pursuit not always as charmed as maybe we would have liked to have believed....
Even though once upon a time in Edinburgh the festivities were fine... And a whole time locked spasm of politically-tortured-terror... Had dragged-up
my maliciously maligned mind.... Downbeat into an era of unforeseeable error...

Bad Khats on my case and I was out to escape.......
Escape the error of ever letting the evil of somebody else's hatred ever relate it's xenophobic venom too my own....

I mean....I'm vicious enough as it is.......

But then hope...Yeah ! There is hope.......
I mean.... I pray from Time to Time ....
& from Time to Time I rise ....
Above it all...And I was surfacing
from the depths of thier hell ...
And doing quite well at that Time ....

To me in my state of mind this little episode could only have been some sort of abstracted lesson on the folly of complacency.

The horn section in my mind's ear blurted "Barreh Duh-duh Dhu-Dhu-Duh.......!!!!!!!" Like Gabriel or was it Buddy Bolden; whatever it had a sort of finality to it.

The Lady who had collapsed and died had been carrying some luggage...
O.K. So aint we all.? Yeah ! I guess so. But
I mean.... She was on a journey / going somewhere / either coming home from
...or going to a holiday..Who knows ?
All that we knew is that where she ended up
She probably didn't need luggage anymore.

The Kid started to write feverishly.
I borrowed a pen and started to jot down my own messages from the Id.

Death had turned up at the end of the carnival and burst our collective balloon like a demented memento-mori..

And wearing a hangover...Wearing a hangover and
a self-satisfied grin
Glazing the sun drenched Glasgow afternoon with
a thin
yet ever so effective coating of grim as in 'Reaper'.

Death.
I began to ponder...
Mine is inevitable
As is everybodies
And as such refined by Time .

Mine is designed to help me find that without
which
The evil is blind...Yeah ! Evil is it's own blindness
That which can not see me can not reach me
                              Can not defeat me
And all the time I'm thinking of the evil-arsed Hill
Billybastards that are after me.

A wiseman once told me something in a round
about sort of way...
Well . I forget what it was now
I mean ...What could I say ?
I was into : Life / Love / Learning / and Language...
But surrounded by: Dreams / Daring / Damage and
Death....

And it was all happening amidst sultry Angels...
I'd been surrounded by Angels
Hip Angels...
And reached by their capable parallels

And culpable parables.

Eyes / lips/ and lives like jewels
And all in relation to the word renewal
I mean ...Do we consume Life or are we Life's fuel.

I mean.... Have you ever considered George
Clinton's phrase;
"The fear of being eaten by a sandwich'...?
Me ...I can't help it. I'm self reflexive.
Lifes like that.
Or then again Life likes that
And even some Life forms like it !
Either way shit happens.
Deep shit.......

I mean...O.K. Maybe I'm a conscious dude ...? Maybe
I'm not ?
All I'm saying is simply... I know when I'm babbling
shite
And I do it anyway
I mean... Its functional / therapeutic / cathartic...

Poetry to get your shit together by
It's part of my appetite
The fear of being eaten by a sandwich
And the shit was deep.

Yeah ! Heavy-shit...
And after a week of hit & miss
I realised it was hit after hit
I'd tried and transcended
the Time-warped Drool-Skool

I drifted into the realms of the incomprehensible
World of the semiotic
As I floundered for words to describe the linguistically unrelatable
Amidst a maelstrom of
'Related and Unrelated Vibes'
Take Five! Right !
OK... Imagine an imploding yet orgasmic cerebral experience
Its difficult I know... But at the Time
Stardust
Bliss
And a kind of misplaced Hey Miss !
Placed with a Tardiss Kiss
Seeking refuge from the lord of the dawn
Weathering the mindless storm of the weather-worn....And...

I mean....Headcase / Beardshorn....... Night-time-Nightshift-Mentalism
And a Revision of eyes in shimmering blue stardust..

Synchronicity of the Id cathexis kind
Helping me discover my mind despite my libido
Which was trying to provoke a bout of Judo ...
With a definite no-no...
Who fell in love with me as she watched my enthusiasm grow
Was it penis envy or just my Negro-ego...
I guess I'll never really know

I mean.... All I know is I was in deep !

And in deep-deep / Somewhere deep within my sub-conscious mind I could hear Public Enemy's Chuch D declaim in a Hip-Hoppy sort of attitudinal whine ...
" Uh Hu ! Don't yuh know ? Don't yuh know ?"

As I stumble groping my way around the streets of the mind
The back-streets of Edinburgh
Breaking away from the alley-ways of the blind
I find that when ever I get on a role
I end up thinking in rhyme
And it's just my way of trying to breath with my mind
Amidst the smoke from the gunshots
And the violent Shitkickers, smog and the grime
And the sad people stealing my new jeans
(Levi 501's)
Off the washing line
Taxi to the dole will I make in on Time

And why is it that Blaknuss is somehow related to crime....
And buddy can you spare a dime....
And will I be a poet till the end of Time

And Time & Sssspice...The Meaning uf Life...
And Time & Spice & The Meaning uf Life...
And Time & Spice & The Meaning uf Life...

But like I said to the policeman.

Officer it's just Life but probably, not as you know it..
Life...
But probably not as you know it.

I mean you might have some kinda perspective or ideological framework that gives you an insight or some kinda angle on it...
But in general it's probably not as you know it...
No.............................
Probably   not   as   you   know it...
The Meaning of `life ... But not as you know it...
The Meaning of `life ... And some notes on the Space Rhyme Continuum
But probably ....
Probably not as you know it ....
Time and Spice...& The Meaning of Life....
And a whole bunch of stuff...
But probably not as you know it...

At The Party.

At the party someone left the cake out in the rain
But it rained roses
Red, white, yellow, tangerine and pink paper like
petals
Fluttered in the evening breeze
So nobody noticed
So it didn't really matter
Amidst the language of life, love and laughter
And happy ever after.

Never the less the Avenger
Time stood looking
Over my right-hand shoulder
Talking to me
About the heroic third participant
I mean Me ?
Well I just listened / looked / acted like I
understood
Whatever sense I'd have made of it
At that instant
At that moment in time
Would have done me equally as good.

I sat lost in thought composing an ode to a
transcendent saxophone.
My memory dressed for the part in an African tie-
dye suit
the colour of ...my old school's tie, call it night sky
Add a purple velvet bow-tie and then "Like hey call

me ! "
"Call me..."
"Mr"... Nice guy ...? Me ?

God's got Women's intuition. Open up your heart
and listen.
God's got Women's intuition. Open up your heart
with vision.
It's all about your inner tuition, Angel...
Angel !

You wore a black dress and a blue aura
As you sat sedately cross legged at the centre of my
minds eye
A jive-samba let fly a rare Yusuf Lateef flute solo
You swung bolo
As around your feet yapped a little mutt called
Toto

I watched from an upstairs class-room window
Liverpool Collegiate Believe it or leave it
Lattice-work triptych lead-lined diamond glass
Navy-blue stars in the sky
Blurry eyed night class
Mirror from the depths of the past
Vous mon cher, mais oui ! Voyeur at the bottom of
sea
Well You did ask
Time flies fast..."But why me ?" the mind boggles
You merely bask.
Your bewilderment buried Like some long
forgotten dream

Along with a Blues based grave yard scene
And a picture stolen from the beginning of
another college scenario...
Like a like a like a
Vision in stereo
And all I could say was "Yeah ! Yuh know !"

Funeral white flowers
Decorated by a vendetta.
You sang an aria
Accompanied by
The photograph of a cello
United powers met the air was mellow
And Je ne regret rien
But then again that was then.
But never again.

Never against my better judgment
For I lost my reputation for good taste
Or was it merely just my taste for good reputation

God's got Women's intuition. Open up your heart
and listen.
God's got Women's intuition. Open up your heart
with vision.
It's all about your inner tuition, Angel...
Angel !

From a grave-yard scene In New Orleans
Inscribed in the language of
A visual Batucada
I faded and reappeared
Wearing a sequined harlequin's mask of varying

hues
Just in time for the masked ball
Enchanted by your spell
But leaving no clues.
I simply pretend to be amused
By a name that only you would call…

You as precious as a piece of
Antique Afro-Cuban jewelry
And you thought you knew me
But if Love is a pearl then Life is a Creole casserole
Laced with emeralds spiced with ruby.
And if music Truly be the Food of Love
Then let me wear it's multi- coloured Gris-Gris
rhythms
As the Jesterley ribbons of my most Sacred Fool's
motley.

Diamond by design my disguise
Became harder
While you triggering a trap
You sprung yourself
Became ensnared as you enraptured
Captured by the coolness
Of the warm-night air
And that something special that made you say
In your own sweetly-unsophisticated yet sadistic
way
"I just don't care.
Trick or Treat / Do or Dare
I'm going to have to go there…
Where ever it may lead".

Eyelashes plead
A sigh designs a snare
Silver web spun glistening
Clinging lace embroidered dream
Transparent sanguine chalice spilt
To gild the heart with blood and guilt
Yet neither of us were want to bleed...

Helplessly bound by the derision
Implicit within your wanton decision
I can only listen to your need
And before either of us had time to really take heed...
There you were without a care
Dusky English rose composed of metal petals...
Polished, relaxed, and in full control you settle
As you affect the exotic dialect of an Andalusian muse.
Fashioning speech from musical notes   that floated
Upwards from an ocean Of Soul.

You underlined the feeling with an ancient wisdom
An obscure logic that I've forgotten now
As much as you had even then.

God's got Women's intuition. Open up your heart and listen.
God's got Women's intuition. Open up your heart with vision.
It's all about your inner tuition, Angel...

Angel !

I recede submerged in the mystery of your
imagination
Low key, quill in hand, oudh at my side, parchment
on my knee
Trying to bridge an affinity
(as an antidote)
To your pre-minstrel asymmetry
Allowing you to question me
Openly and Freely
I am allowing you to question me openly and
freely
But you can not see me clearly
But you still can not see me clearly...
And the sounds you make can only be described as
Give me a word ?
Originally I'd chosen "Uneasy"
Later to be replaced by "Sleazy".

Merely a line I offer by way of evasive explanation
As I peruse the possibilities
Of a life-time of
Perpetual Lexical Procrastination
An endless serendipitous education

My pockets are empty but my heart is full
But what does it matter if you can not see the
moon
Because your ears are dulled
To the Blue Notes of a Marabout from Moorish
Spain

Or the Sufi Soul of a Troubadour codex from Aquitaine
Wherein the Name and the Naming
Are always other than the Named
In the Heart of Hearts where all song is plain
Love rains. Love reigns. Love Reigns.

Speaking over my left-hand shoulder at a reflection
Of the original offender I meander around your innuendoes
To redress a casual yet causal slander As I stake my objection !
"Stay thy hand Avenger ! "Recognize the signs
The Juggling Clown keeps a watch on the time
Let us not preempt the final designation of roles
For whatever our destinations
A highway-man lays in wait
To way-lay our surest goals.
But this time This time is for fun ! The Music is fine.
And Love's clichés they flow like sparkling wine
The music is fine and Love's cliches they flow like wine
And the Party's just begun,
The Party's just begun
This Life has just begun....

Masque.

In Africa they say the warriors mask is the hardest to take off

You removed mine with no apparent effort what
so ever.

Piece by piece my armour and my armoury fell
away
With each memory …Of that moment.

Now I am trapped in this prison I call "Longing".

Zen Poet.

My stuff was once described as;
"A Litany of Life, Love and Laughter",
Albeit by myself.
Never the less it remains true to this day. :-)

As serendipity would have it… I
once reinvented myself as a Zen poet…
Quite by accident.
Like racou it kind of just happened.

I was seeking out fresh poetic inspiration
And my Uncle Omray Roberts said to me
"Wales man ! Look You ! Wales ! Isn't it !".

So I booked a caravan for an aquaintance,
and myself,
in
Llanfairpwllgwyngwllwryndrobwynllantsiliogog
ogoch.

Llanfairpwllglwnngwllwynndrobwnllantsiliogog
ogoch

What a wonderful town there's a train station, pub, a church, and public phone box. The name stretches out till the next train stop.

      So nice they were gonna name it twice
Until one of the committee suggested that
They may have actually done that already.

      And as my aquaintance, and I strolled through leafy glades
I was tuning into the crazy improvisations of the wind in the trees, and the babbling brooks...
My aquaintance turned to me and says;
"Why did you bring me here ? You know I don't do outdoors."
But I couldn't hear her.
The inspiration of being amongst Nature was filling me up
With creative Chi energy...
And I said to her; "Babe your eyes are like a mystic ocean"
      And as if she could feel the Kundalini energy rising up in me ...
Call it telepathy
Call it Women's intuition
Call it Zen
Call it Drishti
Call it a Joycian epiphany
Call it an indescribable moment of Jungian synchronicity
Call it what you will...
She looked me in the eye and whispered in her own

inimitable way
"You're really full of it tonight aren't you."

It was a rhetorical question.
No need for a question mark.

I just thought, "What it is ! Is what it is baby !"
Kismet.

And as I was strolling along crooning "Llanfairpwllgwyngwllwryndrobwynllantsiliogo gogoch a hell of a town baddap bap-bap barra barra badaap !".
I was having trouble trying to make it scan as a song
So in the end I just wrote;
"I   was   in Llanfairpwllgwyngwllwryndrobwynllantsiliogog ogoch".
Scrapped the song idea, and just called it a haiku.

My first haiku and it was mostly in Welsh, "How cool's that ?".
Actually it was closer to a Senryu than a haiku.
But like hey who'd know outside of Japanese literary circles.
Apart from yours truly of course.

And that's what tipped me over into the Zen headspace.
Just one Senryu / oblique stroke / Haiku
An inspired act that was no more than a spontaneous reaction

To the exasperatingly long name of the place we were staying in.

Never the less it turned out to be just one Zen moment too many.
From then it was a slippery slope.
My poetry just got more and more minimal.

As I ambled through woodland glade I spotted this gnarled-up old oak tree...
Roots all matted like a six month old set of weave extensions.
And I thought "Oh mighty Oak !".
And I waited for the next line to come, but it never came.
And I thought that's all I need to say.
That says it all. I see it now … "Oh mighty Oak !"

It was like another Joycian epiphany.
There was a Basho-like succinctness to the whole expression
Like it had truly been a product of no-mind.
And from that one non-thought my career as a Zen poet was born.
I called that first Zen Tree poem 'Ode to an Old Oak tree'.

After that it was like I'd hit on a formula.
By the time we got back to the B&B
I'd composed my first slim volume of Zen minimalist tree poems.
Entitled 'Trees I have Known and Loved',
Which I published under the pen name Wu Wei.

Then there was the wantonly alliterative
'Ode to a Wimpish Willow tree';
"Oh ! Willow weeping Willow. Wimp of the
woodland glade".
A tad verbose in comparison
But as a John Clarian homage it kinda worked
As I thought it cameoed my sensitive side.

Then I was inspired with the controversial
'Ode to a Pine Cone';
'"Oh pine ! Fresh pine ! ".
That was the one people said sounded a bit
commercial.
And that was the one that Jeyes Cleaning Fluid
tried to sue me over.
In the end they agreed to settled out of court.

Then after witnessing some wayward
scallies
Wantonly tossing coke cans
Into a pristine crystal stream.
I was inspired with 'Ode to the Birch'
Which was truly mystical
Given that there were no birch trees in plain sight
It just seemed appropriate at the time.
It went ;
" Oh Birch ! Bring back the birch".

A well known literary critic
Who shall remain nameless
Accused the poem of betraying an excess of Yang
energy in its composer.

My response was 'Ode to a Birch part Two':
The Big Yin version;
" Oh Birch. Beautiful yet brutal. You brute U. You Beaut U."

Then there was the Rumiesque perplexity of 'Ode to a Yew Tree'.

A veritable palindrome of a poem that reads the same backwards;
"Yew ! U yew U ! Yew !".
One critic accused it of being over simplistic.
I bumped into him once at a poetry festival
And all I could think to say to him was:
"Why you ! You ! YOU !"
A reviewer of my slim volume of Zen tree Poems
Writing for the Zen Weekly described my work as ;
"The art of Writing Poetry, that is Not Writing Poetry".
A seemingly ambiguous statement, but one with which, in that context I was actually quite pleased.

The Dot.

The dot below the Ba.
The I that is not.
The zero that makes not being
Be all that it's possible to become.

Each Soul a rose

A fragrant sweet melody to hum
A delicacy with an original flavour
A harmonious chord to strum
An enticing fragrance to subtly savour
An enticing beat from the heart's own drum.

The rhythm of Life in continuous remembrance
Of all that is written … Makhtub!
"Wow! Wow! Wow! Wow!"
All that is to come into being.
"Wow! Wow! Wow! Wow!"

Watan! The Placeless Place.
The unknown space
The future. The unknown country.
The future from where ushers forth
The constant flow of Love's improvisations.

Improvisations enigmatic and mysterious
Detailed multi facetted thought formations
Kalaedoscopic heart vibrations.
Each mind patterned on a comprehensive design.

Polished like cultured pearl overtime
Each Soul impregnated with the Light of the
Divine.
Each in it's right and in it's own time.
"Time! Time! Time! Time!"
The Light!
The Divine! Wijdan (Discovery)!
"Wow! Wow! Wow! Wow!"

See the Soul's glimmer and shine

Shot through with their original natures
"Souls! Souls! Souls! Souls!"
Each Soul shot through with God's original names
Clear and bright the Fitr (Original face)
Self discovery. God's disclosure.

Each dawn we draw a prostration nearer
To the right place
The right frame of mind
The synchronicity that is always on line
The Ever Present Moment!
The Eternal Now!
Hu! Wu! Mu!
Discovery! Discovery! Discovery! Discovery!
IN whose presence we cease to exist
No him! No her! No us! No them! No you! No me!
Only Hu! Only Be!

Soul On Ice.

Average citizenship you know a status denied
Too many stereo-types been invadin' the lifestyle
Give your Ego an inch and you know they'll take a
mile
I mean Network 23 is right now we're on prime
time

Some get through / Some arrive at a place with a
view
Of the new that some how helps them survive
Some thrive / Some strive to keep the Soul alive...
Some spice-up the message and lace it with jive.

Tracin' back through the facts of a modern Black
history
Unwravellin' the tracework of knots in the
mystery
Some structural setbacks accepted and rectified
But the road is long and the struggle is broad and
wide
Like the River Jordan broad and wide

Once recited by the throngs who sang the Gospel
songs
Inspired by the Freedom! For which they longed
Gives a whole new meanin' to the word foregivin'
Through blood stained seasons new reasons for
livin'

Wounded hearts left bleedin' through open minds
Findin' the Oneness of Creation at the dawn of
Time
We rise above it as brothers and sisters
We make a joyful noise and together we shine.

But if you detect a sombre tone
that's cos the rhythm of the Blues is in my Soul
Like the wail of Coltrane's saxophone
Or a moan from Rumi's love sick poems
Billy Holiday oozin' a smooth Blues tone...

Soul on Ice Cold Chillin' to the bone
Soul on Ice Cold Chillin' to the bone
Soul on Ice Cold Chillin' to the bone
Bear with me I like to rock the microphone!

Now I don't get this funky cos I'm an ethnocentric
It's just that I can't swing with a light-weight pop
thang
Another epidemic of media bad-taste
And all the race-hate mongers are hot on the case.

Poets preach, reach and try to teach when they
speak
And Rappers in general don't turn the other cheek
They just speak what they want from a freedom of
will
What I've spoke is no joke it's been known to kill
off
Bad impressions with a lesson that helps Time
heal
I try to deal the ideal with a zeal to be real.

Manipulation of information / Free your mind let
it forage
Cos the name of the game's the application of
knowledge

Songs to builds up a picture that can help people
think
Sometimes Life's over the top...
Sometimes... It's there on the brink...

But if you detect a sombre tone
that's cos the rhythm of the Blues is in my Soul
Like the wail of Coltrane's saxophone
Or a moan from Rumi's love sick poems
Billy Holiday oozin' a smooth Blues tone...

Soul on Ice Cold Chillin' to the bone
Soul on Ice Cold Chillin' to the bone
Soul on Ice Cold Chillin' to the bone
Bear with me I like to rock the microphone!

A lorra people in the West have looked elsewhere
For a place in the Sun or a reason to care.
In places we were never taught ever existed
When I discovered the truth I must admit I felt
twisted

I went inward and reflected tried to stay objective
I knew I had to solve it cos it couldn't be neglected

I dug the sound of some Sudanese Sufi's on a
mountain top
Ramadhan mid-night chantin' Surahs non-stop...

Soundin' like Roots Rock Reggae,
Afro-Jazz, or some avante-garde Trip-Hop,
Drank it into me Soul to the very last drop

See I couldn't refuse it so I just Rhythm & Bluesed it
The feel was Global & Holistic so I knew I had to
use it
It had been there in my blood like a skin-tight fit
Runnin' through my veins and now I'm conscious
of it
And as a Blues wail cuts a path through thin air
It sounds to me like the call to prayer.
In retrospect I reflect and it's all quite clear...

Somethin' I feel that all the people on our lonely

little planet
should know...

Free the song in your heart and the harmony grows
Free the song in your heart and you will feel Love flow
Free the song in your heart and then you will know...

But if you detect a sombre tone
that's cos the rhythm of the Blues is in my Soul
poemsLike the wail of Coltrane's saxophone
Or a moan from Rumi's love sick
Billy Holiday oozin'a smooth Blues tone...

Soul on Ice Cold Chillin' to the bone
Soul on Ice Cold Chillin' to the bone
Soul on Ice Cold Chillin' to the bone
Bear with me I like to rock the microphone!

Haiku #1.

Sodium lamps / Shed lucozade light/ On the rain wet road.

Elements.

And now you walk with Nature...
Free like The Elements.

Forests / woodlands / leaves and trees...

things we need so that we can breath.

And now you walk with Nature...
Free like The Elements.

Waterfalls / rivers and streams...
things that keep our bodies clean.

And now you walk with Nature...
Free like The Elements.

Mountains / hillsides / rocks & stones...
things from which we build our homes.

And now you walk with Nature...
Free like The Elements.

Sunshine / moonlight / lightnings fire...
things that lift the Soul up higher.

Focus.

A ray of incandesance
Pin-pointed with purpose
Premeditated luminosity
In tact & correct.

Such inpenetrable poise can make people nervous
Reality often has that effect.

Exploding the obvious/ Focussed light/ Focussed
light through a lens

In Brignall Crofts in Burmantofts.
I think of you surrounded and alone.

Focussed light !
Focussed light through a lens.

Fresh.

Leaping from the bone-white cliff
into the unsuspecting blueness
I soar
Upwards like a swallow

Riding the warm up-draft
Negotiating the cold cross winds
that drag down into the darkness
of the waters bluest depths

The darkness seethes and the sea breathes
The sea speaks / The sea thinks
The sea leaks / The sea links

A myriad tributaries that feed
Into the warm bloodstream
of this place

Trace it's trajectory
Running with the wind / drinking in the rain
a line / a curve / a wave again
Fresh !

The Zone.

Silver cool the green of Love's garden
Perfumed silk to wrap your heart in...
Verdant pastures of the serene unseen

weaving their way into the most unexpected of
places
the most unexpected of heavenly places.

I am in the Zone / the healing zone
A place close to home / a place with a rhythm all of
it's own.
It is the place where I will meet the Weaponless
Hunter
the Whirling Dancer.
She who must be faced.

Arturo's Hat.

(Poem from a Gladys Mary Coles Work Shop John
Moores Lit. Ba Hons.)

Arturo wore a pork-pie hat
short round and semi-flat.

A middle-aged Cuban-Amerikkkan
Black New York epitaph that lies
in the graveyard of an exiled child.

Grown now to appreciate that
although seperated for years
in retrospect it has become
as clear as cream-soda
that some things are forever near.

And the things we say, do, and wear
all come from somewhere..
deep within our past.

Just a nonchalant nineties fact
that I realise as I catch
a glimpse of myself
in a mirror as I walk past
and notice that I'm wearing
a short round semi-flat
pork-pie hat.
He would have liked that…
By now I'm quite sure of that.

Con-sequential.

A line / a curve / a wave
An eye / a look / a glance

A word / a frase / a chant
A poem / a song / a dance

A sigh / a moan / a prayer-like tone…
a message via telephone

A feather / A wing / a lock of hair
A breath / a breeze / a rush of air

A feeling / a knowing / a sense / an ache
A trickle / a waterfall / a lake.

Jack.

(Poem from a Woardhoard weekend workshop in Huddersfield, with Jack Herscheman.)

Jack came over from San Francisco along with David Meltzer
and Peter Plate. He was an active member of the American Communist Party and did time after time from the fifties, through the sixties, and seventies for his political beliefs.
Now he edited a broad based Left-Field magazine called Left Curve.
He also Translated dissident poetry into English from eight different languages including French Creole, Spanish, Italian and Hatian Patoise.

About a dozen other writers and myself are sat around a table at the Wordhoard in Huddersfield being prepared to write a headshot... A headshot is a stream of consciousness... With Jack it's an exercise that follows about three hours of discourse on projecting the inner-dimensions of the self onto the page.

It's an Indian Summer as they say, 1996. I arrive in Hudds via Cardiff, London, Lincoln, Bristol, Manchester, York, Leeds and Liverpool. It's been along Summer. I'm hyped, restless... But full of expectations.
The state of mind is more of an exercise in "feel good".

I actually feel wounded but on the mend. It's a long story .
You probably wouldn't wanna know.
And anyway at least I feel alive.

I sample and construct my own thoughts around the bassline of Jacks theme...
This anchors the tempo of the groove...
My own personal demons drive the rhythm.
My blood flows red in my viens...
The pulse kicks ...
Jack begins the ritual healing...
"Replenished from the roots...

Living as a juggler I leap through lifes hoops / Keeping open all the possibilities/ Compelled by the Future".

The sounds of my Soul... Streamline what sense I make of all this.
And I am propelled by the sutures in my torn sense of human dignity.
But this also is bliss.

"Control...Is...Is......."
So important...
At this point being who I am...

That which I am
Fool seems a good word although I am loath to admit it

Still something inside me seems to know that

the insolence of the Clown purifies and liberates !

Jack... Of course I understand You...
And in a lot of ways I am you... In a lot of ways.
But at present at this moment... At this point in time... I am... more me...
I mean I'm a Born again Beatnik...from the darkside of Beat City...
The South side...

To me the future isn't always... Isn't always... Insured ?
Insured ? Me ? Moi ? Ha ha ! I'm a predator that sometimes fall prey to pretty superficialities and such as would make warriors weep.

Still... That is ...... I know what your saying and its what I believe in. In part...
...It's what I need to hear... A future ... Open to whats coming... Yeah !

The future thing... Possibilities The beginning of the future... Something new.
Could this be...? I mean unbeknown to you I'm at a place
Where....... I'm starting new.......

The sense of the future- Jack preaches "Hope" I like that

"The future belongs to poor people/poets/and players of instruments " Jack says...

I like that too... "Poetry is the future"... says Jack

"The Perfume of my poverty" he adds echoing The Prophet Muhammad Al Mustafa (Sallallahu allihi wa salaam).

It's also the fresh air of my here and now...

"Je suise trés desolé mon chér
c'est ne pas ma faute...
Il est de l'ambiance. Oui ?
Ma petite fleur
Vous-avez demandé la musique ne quité pas""

Even though at some point in the future
I will reconcile all the madness with the
Idea...
'The Idea / Le bonne idee'.

I mean lets see...
We discuss Pablo Neruda's... Postman
Postman Pat Postman Pat and his Black & White Cat...
And I appear to be the only Black and White cat in a hat that would buzz
On a stupid rhyme like that
So I drop it...

In the future I will write a brief socio-historical note on
Black Devotional Music
and the
Survival, and Transmission of an African Islamic Spirituality
Amongst the Post-Trans-Atlantic Slavery

Diaspora.
I was deep back then or so I thought
At the time.

But for now
Jack says I gotta get to
The me... Beyond the poet... poetics... poetries...
poetry...

The people on the street and in the clubs and
cafés pubs and bars and bistros and snakepits
and sleazy dives alehouses art spaces theatres and
open spaces the public spaces
That I inhabit are all actively poetic...

Everybodies a poet, an MC, a DJ or a comedian...
Potentially...pumping out prosaic prophecies
pulsating with pleas for Peace...
And Please Baby please !
The Blues being a reflection of the ...
Hearts intoxication with that which is ultimately
Toxic.

Gestures - The way we move through life-Our
relations with others....
People are poetic...We exude poetry...All of us in
our own Way...
Especially when we are comfortable enough to feel
at liberty...
To talk freely...
"Are we free to talk ?"

Surfing on the rhythm now...

Opposing the vainglorious superficialities of serfdom...
As seen from above...We swerve... I've got a free-style swerve on...
A Lyrical extension of something else...
A Rap thing kicking with a swing of inspiration...
A little bit Weeerrrrhhh ! A little bit Woooaaahhh !

"Is this a statement or the mere recollection of a particular situation...
How can we as Black people create a statement for the nation
whose nation..." From the Beat-generation to the Hip-Hop Nation
How do we separate nation from state
and state from race... The race from guns... I'm on a run or Am I... On the run?

Jack is urging us to confront our spectres.
the ones that are haunting us here now.
It happens to be part of my philosophy but I hold back
After all it's Jack's workshop.
I make notes and take quotes...

As a simple man...
As the basic underlying principle
Like anybody in my position
I am a... Blues Print.

Oooooooh! Wooo Woo-woo yeah !

Our music is our mother tongue.

A protagonist of antagonistic assumptions...
To some... Certain revelations coming into fruition.
I'm grooving on Jack's intro... The inspiration kicks in...
It's a Jazz dirivitive...
There's a Blackman's vibe in it...
diggin' the flow
There I go...There I go there I go...
I go there...

He speaks the group ...Sparks them !

"Love is the ground of human existence.
Equality is being equal in another's eyes..."

My thoughts drift to you... Babe...You were always White is right in relation to me... My ex-lover... X-rated
Whatever... I can hear Ricki Lake and Montel both saying in unison ...
"Don't even go there !"
So I don't
But like some San Francisco Shaman from the Sixties Beat haven Jack or is it Jazz now... Draws out our demons of rage and traps them on the page.
I can just see him in the Sixties getting arrested for chanting "Out Demons! Out !" Outside the White House burning the Stars & Stripes
In the name of the strugglin classes.

But you. You were allways a class above most

people in your own mind's eye...
Even your own folks.

It wasn't your fault ... Isn't your fault... Your background
Your culture is so fundamentally flawed with delusions of grandeur.

Love is...
Being equal in another's eye's... And... I think of you...
And how you could never really have...or How could you ever really have...
Cold you...
(a typographical error... It seems apt so I leave it in tact)
End of sentence.
Full stop.
New paragraph...stanza / wharever...

What I meant to say was... Could you ever have?
Maybe... Once... Yeah maybe once... Once upon a time...Right ?
And a big fat 'Maybe... Right Baby ?
"Don't go there !" warns Ricki.
"My Nigga Please !" says Montel forgetting his training.

"All poetry is love poetry.
All poems a love poem".
Jack's words...

Short simple statements that I edit.

Short statements to be shot down..
By your ill informed verdict...
Lover. The word stings my lips.

"And Love is... the most dangerous form of politics
that there is..."
My words...

But I know I'll get over it. It's just a question of
time.
Jack chants for us to excede our limitations of
expression.
And we do.
Each in our way.
Each according to our measure.
As is The Way.

"What underlies this is the future.
Sometimes we have to fight for the future"
Jack's words...
My sentiments...

Ok human nature is by it's very definition is a
contradiction of sorts.
A Yin & Yang thang
A play of opposites ...
Your more of a confrontation addict in an
inconclusive
Wild Whirl of a World... Wind of change...

What I produce isn't as bitter as it tastes to some
people.
It's just that in my Rap years I elevated "Dissin" to a

high-art form.
I was an evil bastard. I've mellowed out sort of.

"Roots R.O.O.T.S. to Routes R.O.U.T.E.S."
A theme I've explored before in my own way,
interesting that it should pop up
Today...
She told me she was from the School of
Synchronicity...
Her madness made me so horney...
But like hey ! Thats poetry and poetry is life or is it
Jazz or just cerebral jizzum...
Am I right ? Come! Come! ... or is it or just "How
come ?"
" You betcha !" says the Beathead at the back of my
mind not even listening...
But Bucking up some Bravado just in case.

Jack or is it Jazz Now... Speaks
"Thought for the day...
Bazookoed by Etymology"

It's intense I escape into a moment of delerium as I
day-dream
At a tangent to the main theme.
If you de-pun Finnegan's Wake you get
Shakespeare
If you pun on de Shakespear you get Shakka's
Spear.
Elizabethan English..Language...Echoic...
Liverpool Echo...Echo !...Echo !...

Shakespear was a Sufi poet.

Symptom's of a Jazz attack or just Jack's workshop
He's triggering people left-right- & centre...

Naming words that have existed inside us...
Words we have never done anything with...

The room is pulsating with energy.

"Delerius trees of delerio dendron" says Jack

Rhododendrons and their wildly uncontrollable
roots
Something you taught me about babe... I
remember...
Remembering... Reborn... Into the pain...
Pursuing Pleasure... Reborn...replenished...
Beginning a new I remember...You.
(Frank Ifield eat your heart out).......

What are your favorite words: Je Jeune says "Jack"...
J is for ...JaZZ
Jack speaks and it all sounds like poetry.
Kinda Jazzy Kinda flowy... Kinda yuh knowy...
Then he makes a reference to me
"Muhammad-Eugene has just finished his
masters..."
A map reference...pour moi...

Something that marks the instance...
This moment...
This point in time.

My assault on academia merely an act of rebellion

for me...
A move against those... or that which would keep
the likes of me down...
In ideological captivity...intrinsically...
Those who would arrest my developement...
restrict my growth...cramp my mobility
Not of any premeditated sense of malice merely in
order to fulfill
A self fulfilling prophecy of their own...

Back to you babe...
Ricki throws her arms around Montel. Hugs him.
He kisses her on the forehead. They watch with
bated breath.

Yeah baberrr ! back to where your at..
Where you are...
Where your coming from...
Where are you ?
Love and all that...Love and All that...Good stuff...
The where you are the town your in all making
new meaning for you... But what ?

We name things... Sometimes.. You can't...
Sometimes.. It's not possible...
Sometimes we need more than the sounds of
words...
Still we name things...
From out of something... that is naturally a part of
us.

"The ether of intelligence".

Something Jack sees in the English...
He includes me in "the English" as he tells us this...
He's out to destroy that which he sees as The English in us...
This assists me in agreeing with him... In part...

"The revelations of rationality reduced to rants of absurdum at times".

Stuff like this starts flying around the room.
I catch some of it and decide to decypher it later.

As memory energizes... mysteriously mesmerises...
Me, Jack, Aggie, Keith, Diane, Steve, Akwa, Neil... the whole posse...
We... take off on a Dyonesian Odyssey...
Apolonian in its abstraction...
A bardic sumtin'...cathartic in its contradictions...
Total... Tao Oneness ! Tauhid ! Tewahado !

Jack goes off on one. He's like an MC Freestyling in Kabbalah
Springing something loose from the juice... touching those chords...
It gets kinda X-Filey

"Voices/Beacons/ Pressing forward/the stress that is the tension/ of time travel...
Antennae will emerge spirit time travelling from the 20th Century
to the 21st Century " Beacons of spiritual... insight and forsight...""

Jack's words...

"In the light of that which is dark...That which will not go away..."Mine...

All of us... We work in combination...
Like linguistic sextractions
Hands on ambiguity
French symbolism
Oral realism
Pump action poetry...
Defying the all too real gravity of The Situation.

It gets incestuous.
I'm trying to sort some baggage from a recently deceased relationship...
As mentioned...
And I bask in the warmth ...
And the temporary closeness.
Rebound Therapy I call it.
This time I don't think of you.
This time I think of somebody I met briefly in Cardiff.
Montel & Ricki are on my case. Who was it ?
It doesn't matter who it was.
The soap opera stagnates.

"The real energy of poetry...
To place yourself in that which is already...
Fighting... for existance...
Literature... In the accepted sense...
Of the word...
That is traditionally...

In terms of... that which is considered to be...
The literate in an academic sense...
I must add...
Is dead...
or at least held in bondage by leather bound
bookworms of distinction..."

It starts to get a little bit anal...
Liberate these brothers and sisters from the
Vainglorious egotism...that they parade as
valour...
I think to myself as I imagine...
Veiled references to our voluptuous revelries
Baby...as you burn remember to tell your aid de
camps.
Air conditioned graceless associates that I have
premonitions
Relating to your collusions with the
fundamentally flawed aristocracy
Of snake nobility and fake sensibilities.

I spit out poison sucked from out of the wound
where I was bitten.
Ricki & Montel are fucking at this point, but ever so
discretely.
The yanks love this kinda thing.

The real energy of Poetry belongs to those who are
Hungry for it...
Hungry equals angry...
And I make no apologies for the taste of my rage if
its flavour is bitter

On the back... of your throat... Then swallow.
For callow as I am I would not like you to choke...
Compassion is at the heart of my rage
As I spill the seed of my wrath onto this pristine
Ever so clean sanitized page.
Why-tear than white...

"I purge my soul of any adulterous allegiance to
any flag..." says Jack
Or have I just made that bit up.
It doesn't matter at this point.
The heat is blistering.
I howl at the moon...The one you love to dance
with...
Listen !...
They're playing with our song...
Of course not like we did... cello... basoon... flute
and of course darabukka...
I sing Bobby McFerrin's version of Van Morrison's
Moon dance.
In a polyphony of oscillating keys that were really
just
The Key of X ...
And we danced...

A red scarf tied to the end of my lance...
As I ride towards...
As if I knew...
You don't know what you gonna do...
And here I am talking as if anyone knew...
What they were gonna do..
Let me try to articulate...

Saying...Trying...Saying...
Trying...to get to the Heart...
of the Total dimensions of emotion...
Jacks quest. The exercise he has set.

Jack throws in some more stuff...
"The confrontation of possibility.
The possibilities of confrontation.
Look at my page...I am that page...
Something upon which you can project yourself.
A field of energy.
A construct.
A place where a transferance of energy
Continually takes place...
Supposed you looked at the page..."

Poetry is the language of the Human Heart...
And this is where the Soul lives...
But "always keep one door closed" said Aggie...
I have to agree...
I know people who have bled to death from such folly...
As the wearing of sleeves that expose too much tenderness...

After all anticipation is said "to be 90% of the pleasure in sex"...
Adds Jack...
And the Heart that rages against injustice... Does so in whatever it does...
and it is most sincere when raging on it's own behalf...

This to me is common sense...
Of sorts...Isn't it...I mean tell me if it isn't...

Aggie says "The rage is what's interesting"
"Reading the newspapers is like reading the Thieves Journal" says Jack "The dialogue is what's interesting.
Male and female/internal and external Yin and Yang".
"Love, sexuality and socialism" says Jack...
"India rubber ball" replies Aggie...
This is poetry...
There is melody in it...
Sibilance...
A music.
"If your a poet your in love with sound" says Jack ...
I agree in my own mind...

He continues...
"I was driving along with Aggie and she says...she likes to do something with Jazz. Sing!...Move with Jazz...""Where is the Jazz is England"
Jack asks...
"I know !" I think to myself...
"You've mentioned it already ...You've mentioned where..."

We break for coffee...Aggie fills my cup...Well nearly...
I get up to add milk and sugar
Fragmenting the group... Seep... into the room where the coffee is...

As we all break for coffee...
"Is this lunch or coffee break" asks Charlie...
Who has been writing but is too shy to show her thoughts...
Tortured the expression on her face...
I am curious...
She looks...Serious...Silent...Still...
As she pensively persues a memory
Studious as she peruses her page of confrontation...
Her projected spectre of rage...
We are here now...The struggle continues...
My words come to me...
The ones I don't do
enough with...
A luta continua...The struggle continues...
Is...
A small one after the word "Is ! " indicates a footnote.
I shift my gaze to the accompanying footnote and read...
It says... Sulook
"Journey Home".

The Tape Blues.

Yeah ! Free me up... Talking 'bout the Tape.
I need to talk about this tape bro !

The Tape was crushed ice in a desperate situation
The mystical warmth of mountain-top meditations.
It was no hesitation / Shere dedication
It even had a version for the radio station.

I mixed in screams and gunshots from the television.
Scene's from the razor's edge and some split decisions.
It was a panoramic vision / under special supervision
Laced with various sardonic shades of man on a mission.

The Tape was Slick ! The Tape was Baad !
The hit on that Tape was where it's at !
The Tape was dope ! The Tape was fly !
The underground bits that you just can't buy !

It was a hardcore tone from a dodgy postal zone.
A subliminal text set in skull and crossbones.
It was a rhythmic ride run on dignity and pride.
It was the might of the Mersey swelling at full tide.

And the nearer it got to it's main objective.
All generic criteria became ineffective.

As the Tape honed in on it's main directive.
It was totally unique and subconjective.

The Tape was Slick ! The Tape was Baad !
The hit on that Tape was where it's at !
The Tape was Dope ! The Tape was Fly !
The Underground bits that you just can't buy !

The Tape was the day / the Tape was the night
From the darkness of the Tape showed forth the light.
Words that burst the bubble of bourgeois illusion.
Bringing clarity to inarticulate confusion.

The tape was impolite with a beat that bites
It was a blue light that self-ignites.
It was raw rocket fuel uncut and crude.
It was infuriating up to the point of rude.

The Tape was Slick ! The Tape was Baad !
The shit on that Tape was where it's at !
The Tape was dope ! The Tape was fly !
The underground bits that you just can't buy !

The tape was laced with the light of nothing left to loose.
The realisation that everybody got the right to choose.
Like the rage in the veins of the underdog's struggle.
The type of Blues that talks itself in and out of trouble.

The Tape was chanting, romancing, Spirit dancing

Midnight prancing and Ocean glancing...
Cos the Tape was deep and the Tape was fizzy
The Tape was busy, and the Tape was dizzy.
It even had a verse about my Aunty Lizzie.

With a Hi-brow glow / And a Lo-brow diss.
There was never a session that kicked like this.
But someone left the Tape out in the rain
I don't think that I can take it
Cos it jammed-up when I tried to play it
And I'll never vibe that flavour-flow again.
Oh No !

That's why I gotta talk about the Tape my brother...
I gotta talk about the Tape... Cos....

The Tape was Slick ! The Tape was Baad !
The hit on that Tape was where it's at !
The Tape was dope ! The Tape was fly !
The underground bits that you just can't buy !

The Tape was Slick ! The Tape was Baad !
That Scallywag shit was where it's at !
The Tape was dope ! The Tape was fly !
The underground shit that you just can't buy !

Haiku #2.

Grey Mist enhances
The rolling majesty of
The River Mersey.

Kew Gardens Sufi Arts Fest.

The time has come for Love
The time has come for Unity

Al Wadud wa al Hubb wa al Ishq !

For the Ummah-The Community-The Sufis
Are here for all to see
They come from all Humanity
Every racial divide every taste every country
From continental shelves and village streets
Islamic creativity and it's all free
Exotic Fresh Prosaic and Pretty
Love wins roses for the inner city jinns
Hearty laughs and toothy grins
The rhythms of Eternity
Spires without enmity
Spies without enmity...

The time has come for Love
The time has come for Unity

Al Wadud wa al Hubb wa al Ishq !

Prelude to a Pirate Utopia.

When such obscure compositions as Erwinn
Schulhoff's
'Bass Nighting gale' have become household names
And everybody is familiar with the sound of the
Berimbau/Or the bongo mix of Rule Brittania

When little old ladies in Victorian tea rooms share
tales of off-beat-off the wall Jazz Griots and Pirate
Utopias
Over a cup of the finest blend
And illegitimate pidgeon-holes are avoided
Like the farcical roles most often acted out
By and in the stiflingly solubrious
Dystopias of the sub-urban mind.

Here we will find our poetry/our art/our culture/
our past and future.
In the most unexpected of places.
The most unexpected of places.

From the savannah grasslands of West Africa
To the wastelands of the UK Jazz diaspora.
In the compacted / collapsed time zone of an as of
yet unknown head-space.
An as of yet enigmatic emission
Emanating from what we could call the urban
present
If we we're to be so glib, so cliche·
So kitch.
The... A Place beyond the vacuous, and the vacuum
Of all that we wantonly consume
In our quest for access to the excess of the getting-
wilder/ West..
An ideological   vacant lot / an attitude that
separates the haves and the have nots...
A time / A place / Where...and When the concept
of identity has become a...Redundancy...So they
say so they would have us believe...

History a thing of the past...or so they say
And... culture a place where recycled signs are distilled /
And seasoned to taste...

On MTV an illiterate minstrell sings dayglow in an American accent...while on another channel all natural colour is drained and refined to a toned down pastel.
As Europe Unites...White on White. In places forming a patchwork quilt of uncertainty, about the word 'we'.

Here you will find my name spray canned on a museum wall in matt-black... scratched across a Picasso with a cuticle remover or carved in the frame of a Tintoretto... with an Apache arrow head.
Somewhere in the Louvre.
Quelle bon idea. Je suise tres desolee, c'est n'est pas ma faute. C'etait... l'ambiance sauvage et le parfum des temps at de Paris a cette epoue. Oui?

Here you will feel my presence in the room.
Smell the sweet, almost acrid fragrance of sandalwood perfume.
Hear my voice attempt an atonal Jazz tune.
"A Love Supreme! A Love Supreme! A Love Supreme"
Allah Supreme !

More power than a panther far sweeter than song
Perfume for the soul makes the heart grow strong.

Let me wear the Zen inherent in the Izness of it all
as a ceremonial sarong
For... performing my Tai Chi after a cup of
Cardommon Tea.

You may see my face peering from out of the
shadows
And possibly if it is in your nature trace the cause
of my inertia
...before its too late.

In the subliminal depths of this semiotic
underground / somewhere
Amidst the congealed entrails of the industrial
revolution and the fossilized remains of The
Empire...
New origins...will have emerged...have and will
emerge...are emerging...
Merging...
Soulful Survivors thriving and Emerging from...
Beneath the bureaucratic Cracker excrement of the
trans-Atlantic slavetrade.
Free formed redefined and warm.

Liked micro-waved food-but more normal
The sweat from a rave but more formal...
Organically growing out of the inevitably
changing energy of the mass.
Organically growing out of the inevitability of
change.
Originating amongst the misplaced plagiarisms of
imperialist-poppy cock.

Popularist haut couture coerced into a
meaningless melange of purile propaganda .
Reducing all potentially progressive protagonisms
to a pap
To pad out the pay-packets and pockets of the
puppeteering perpe-traitors
Of an impotently penis pulling pop-culture.
Oh Yeah !

In the red nosed glow of a rose coloured dawn
Thorns
Decorating the horizon of traditional awareness
Like the Gypsy tents of... Neocentric Nomads.
Nomads from Womad
Eclectic souls with esoteric tastes.
A Saturnalian-Mardi Gras in the Greenwood
The Life Quest continually caught up in life's
carnival essence.
Carnivalessence ? Hey ! Carnivalesque flow !

Cultural mutations playing as they multiply in
hearts and minds of
Sincere Souls plying their art
Into a rainbow of infinite variety a bouquet of
human possibility.
An evolutionary overflow of Omni relational I.D.'s.

Transcending the tedium and the terror of their
t.v.sets
Secure only in the knowledge of all that is
inevitable
An idea whose time has come to pass.

It all warps the clarity of the vision once it has been in the hands of men for a while...
This is reality my sisters and brothers...And it doesn't try and be anything it just is...What it is...

What it is. Its not that easy to say...
Its not that easy to see...You can not describe or see...The invisible pregnancy of all that could be........waiting to be born...All that is waiting to take form...
In an anti-natal World/ where the only genetic norm is/ has ever been mixed race...Origins filed under/ difficult to trace...or belonging to everbody...For as the Redman says "We are all related..."

My country is a place where words like 'Purity' become synonymous with 'Plastic'
And the average voice melts...into a fractal of Creoles, patoises, the N-Word and
Other outlawed linguistic devices / slangs / back slangs / bagarrah gaygack-slaygangs/ argots/ and colloquial twangs that ring with the attitude of dissent...
Decolonised accents become as sacro-sanct...as be-bop scat...hip-hop and rap they go on & on & on & on & they don't stop...
Interbreeding...
A place where meaning is ebullient / eloquent in it's elasticity / erudite in its absurdity...the only absolute / being one of eccentricity...
And language / language leads / language

leads...only to where you believe you can go...
A time when it becomes self evident that
the past was a figment of someone elses
imagination...

From this cascading waterfall of cultural diversity
This salsa of miscegenation
A nation within and beyond the present limits of
the allowed scope for imagination.

and the struggle to impose
meaning..
"A Love Supreme A Love Supreme A Love
Supreme A Love Supreme A Love Supreme A Love
Supreme..."

Angel.

Whatever had been hanging in the air
between us
imploded
leaving a vacuum
that drew us
into the same
space...

Blinded
I traced the symmetry
of your face
the Grace...

Of Him whose beauty glorifies the rose... triangles
softened by curves...

There is an elegance in the fall of Autumn leaves.

The Spark
the Chemistry was there from the first eye
contact...
I could feel it.
There is an elegance in the fall of your hair.

The air crackled between us...
streaks of silver and gold flashed fissures in the
surrounding atmosphere.

Before I knew it my lips
were suspended inches from an Angelic face.
Crackling electric.

But words escaped me...

The vision I beheld blew away all mind...

All meaning leaving only a feeling
of lightening...

A rumble like distant thunder.

Your essence filled my imagination
now swollen from the dancing of invisible
energies.

As a safety measure
I siphen off the excess emotional content of my
heart
into the flask of poetry.

My dreams sizzling into the moonlight darkness.

Spooks.

You may notice...
It may seem dhat we are dancing...
To an inaudible beat...
But what you see is feet dragging...
held back by invisible chains...
aching feet slowed down by invisible
lanes...

Invisible Diasporans...
Doing our own peculiarly
Invisible... Ghost Dance...

Apparitions and spectres scream for mercy
In apparantly inaudible zombie tongues.

Tongues tied to a commodified stammer
Doomed to be spoken in a disposable manner.
Our sense of self ethnically cleansed
Of any meaning that may be relevant to us.
Now that's spooky !

Invisible Diasporans...
It may seem dhat we are dancing.

Rumba Love.

What makes Cuban music
some of the best red hot
music in the world ?

Let's articulate eloquently
at the speed of rhythm ,
the sensuality of sound...

And when we can do that
then we will know.

Blue Light.

Light Upon Light
Deep within the Silence unfolds
Forever young
Forever old.

Shining Soul Fire
Akin to and kindling
Of a burning desire

The Light that can only enter a heart
Through Love's wound.
Encapsulated in sound.
Whatever goes around comes around.

Beyond the Long Night of the Soul
A sunlight far more radiant than gold
Lays beneath the half that's never been told.

Sacred Space.

Let me ignite the incense / Clear the Sacred Space
Sweet fragrance rising / Caressing your face
Slowly dance the hours / Sewing their own seeds
Such delightful flowers / Memories like these.

You Free me…Mama Cita… Oyo ! Mi Corezone !
You Free me…Mama Cita… Cuidado ! Mi Corezone !
You / Free / Me !

In my back yard / Deep roots meditation
My sincerest regards / Grace of sweet inspiration
Just your breath as my rhythm / Making time
stand so still
Purple heart black ribbon / Call it love's
transcendent will

You're like Ocean –Glancing… You're like Mid-
night-Prancing…
You're like Deep Space-Trancing…You're like
JaAaAaazZz Dancing…
Yeah ! Yeah ! Yeah ! Yeah !

In the depths of each heart beat / The shelter of
Agape's Shrine
Nothing left to complete / The golden sunlight
pines
Let me build you an altar / You can recite your own
myths
I'll try to make it so beautiful / That you just love it
to bits.
You / Free / Me !

Addicted.

Giving up all my addictions was easy enough
Because nothing gets me as high as you
But when I tried to give you up

I was 70,000 shades of Blue.

Air.

Breathin'
the air of another
time...

Of reality
sewn together
with dreams...

Remembrance
reinforcing
the seems...

Cafe Bongo.

Yeah! Taking you back in time to Beatnik City to a little place called The Cafe Bongo.

Gonna take a litte trip down town to check out the ease actor at the Please Factory... Some where in the inner-city.

Where a Funky street beat slinks through the night heatDark and discreet as a sleek black panther

A voice sings and is carried on the howling wind...

As if the evening itself is attempting to answer...

 The call of the Cafe Bongo! And it's all at the Cafe Bongo!

All at the Cafe Bongo!

Moonlight salsa and Jazzy sweat salty stars in the sky.

Love this music / Love this music Love/Love this music till I die!

A love sick saxophone that groans as it moans like a Tom-cat

On the hot tin roof of the Cafe Bongo...

And it's all at the Cafe Bongo.

Sneeking down a back-alley paw marks pitter pattering

Over Summer rain wet tiles...

Smiles that slowly fade as the deep patches return to being all one shade...

Totally in Life's flow. Cool & aloof but energetic and slow.

Some say low down low life low grade but never staid

Cos that's the way the game is played at the Cafe Bongo.

Yeah and when people get a little tired they just keep going, Going-going like the bongos.

Two cats leap from the wall to the pavement and onto the street/Without leaving even a trace, or scent or even the slightest dent

Just landing neat leaving no evidence of their deft descent into the hall of the all night heat.

Just the raw truth as proof. The unforgettable point that's been made. Alley cats on a Cafe Bongo night raid.

The type of thing you could call a close shave.

Flashing eyes like spies chattering. High-heels tipped with steel clitter-clattering. Nothin' really mattering.

Time to go - Time to move! Time to see what's happening.

Under cover of the lampless shade shared by the boogie-down arcade where the city people rave.

Rendez-vous are kept/Promises are made/Lovers are lost/Other get paid/Drinks are knocked over/ Lipstick is smudged/ Tie thrown over a shoulder/ Someone else is nudged/Mascara runs...

As the long and the short and the skinny and fat/ Be checking out this thing moving in on that... Jealousies ignite/Games are played/

Relationships abandoned like beds left unmade/ It's like a market place where prices are paid/

Names are sullied or made/Certain guys get OK'd/ Flower dresses disarrayed/Genders displayed/ Poets get laid/The place gets surveyed/Sometimes there's the occasional raid at the Cafe Bongo...

It's just a long walk down a short street

Casually savage but stylistically complete.

Exercise your Jive to a tease factor five or just dig the beat.

As Quincy Jones tickles out a slinky keyboard trickles out a tune form Salango /Two people dance the Tango/ I think it's an Argentinian Malongo/And it's a jungle down at the Cafe Bongo.

Lions/Panthers/Pumas/Bobcats/Tigers/Jaguars/ Lynxes and cougars.

Cats in hats/ Foxes in furs/Minxes in minks/Bimbo brained babes on the brink hanging on to the arm of a Mercedes so rich it stinks/And he's vibing like their in the pussy kitten pink/She's pouting cos that's what they want everyone to think down at the Cafe Bongo.

Home of the tanned actor/Dames dripping in Max Factor/A honeytrap in a bee-hive/Max Factor 5/ High rolling Hi-jinxers/In Satin-Sequins-Laces-Lycra-Fishnets & flounces/Get your ever loving love in by the everlovin' ounces/ They even got some evil looking kick-ass big booted bouncers/ At the place to be where it's/ And it's all just a matter of fact at the Cafe Bongo.

Yeah! So just be yourself for a while and forget the act, cos what it is is what it is and it's like that cos that's the way it is. That's where it's at down at the Cafe Bongo.

No need to worry about being too exact. You can just crazy it up or just chill your will/Max & relax with a sensi direct from Negrille/Sup a pint or sip a sixth of gill/Some sniff powders of drop a mind pop of a pill.

Some fly/Some cry/Some die/Some just get ill...

Some others survive to line up another motherpoppin' kill. If the atmosphere don't get yah then the music sho'nuff will.

At the place to be where it's/And it's all just another everyday matter of fact/The place where the booty and the beats are phat/ And the cool cats wear bad-ass hats/ And when a Rascal licks a shot everybody gets flat.

A deceased Doctor Jive down at the Ju-Ju sanctuary alive direct unchecked and quite satisfactory. I know that you know that he knows that I know cos thats the way it is and thats the way it goes at the Cafe Bongo.

Up town or down town out front or under ground/ People gather round as the ritualistic drums pound out a sound from the heart of creation/

Don't you ever be forgetting Roger Hill's popular music show on the local radio station/ cos it's all at the Cafe Bongo.

August Moon.

The August Moon
Took me on another journey
My harmonica sang
"Don't dare… dare me !"

The Beloved sluices the Heart clean
With the juice of Umbrine.

And she a vaccine of virtual volcanic heat
The Beloved is that from which all Words retreat.

Rose Hips.

My ego swamped with the wine of your smile
I drank from your eyes until I was sick to my Soul
Wouldst that I'd drank from those curling lips
Held you by your womanly hips
But enough of this…I tell myself.

Up North.

Once spoken forever flowing
A whirling surrealism of eloquence
Stitches a watery line between space and time.

An eclectic energy unravelling emotions
Memories / events / cycles / of change
Where culture creates communities.
Creates Grace and fertile ground along the way.

Panoramic visions were clouds form armadas in full sail.
Rolling hill-sides and deep down in the dales.
Like a Blues wail.

A haunted place in parts
where the ghosts of the slave-masters still lurk.
Rusty machinery decorates the landscaped greenery
Where a thriving bee hive of people once worked.
A broken window on the past.
Factories, mills, locks, docks, lime kilns
Sweat shops, shackles and mine shafts.

A too and fro that soothes
Sleuces away the pigeon grey
Taste of soot / grit / broken glass
Carbon monoxide flavoured refried chips.

The eyeline dips
To read the glyphs

Rotted wooden fences
Rusty tin roofs
Throat choking brick dust.

Kids singing "Freedom is a must !"

The torn pages of the post-industrial
Transcript that punctuates
Nay ! Underlines and delineates
The designer lifestyle homelessness
That inhabits the digital present.

The rabid rapids
The filthy flotsam cluttered weir
Improvised music to my ears.
A babbling brook compelling me
To take a look beyond the flawed histories.

As the waters cover the sea
The reflection of an inner reality.

Haiku #3.

Snow storm at mid-night

Comforting the curtains fall

Drawn cross the sky.

Frog Song.

A song gets more strong

Each time that it's sung.

As Frog songs implode
Heavy hearts shed their load.

Tears dissolve fear
And Hearts become clear.

Frog song is the sound of the Blue
Notes that ignite the fuse
Of realising that there is Nothing...
Nothing left to loose.

A Summer Poem.

And when the wind changes, And the moon wanes
the tide will rise and ...I will remember this as
"It was at that time..."

Love's purity of purpose that carries us higher
Than the octopus of our all too human desires
And the times are amazing and the weather's a
jewel
The wind will soon be changing but the vibes are
cool.

The breeze carries the song sung by poets and
peasants
Wolfsheads, dervishes, pirates and knaves
It's the song of the Soul
" No masters. No Slaves."

At Mid-day.

At mid-day I am beginning to make sense of it all
Nature extemporaneously composes works of art
in the sand
As if she was expecting a private viewing
Communicating salt-white the Irish Sea a rose
Grey-brown bronzed shimmering pink
Fragmentation merely a trick of the light

Flagrantly the sun beams salsa through the
swaying pine-tops
Dancing their way into the heart beat of the forest
life
Scattering silken shadows across
Brittle white shells and fibrous brown fircones

Anticipation rises in the blood
Blood in the purple vein
The body ringing with Life's primal aim.

Climbing to the top of the tallest dune
I battle with the wind to get bearings
And in my solitude I practice
A continuity of reinvented memories.

Awakened.

To be alert to things
To consciously engage with Life
Peace is being here
Now I'm focused... clear

No thoughts no emotions no action

Just the sound of your name
Gives complete satisfaction.

The simple charm
Of your feminine presence
That kindles a fire deep within my essence.

More Tea Sister.

The following Saturday my feelings evolved
As I watched the sugar melting in my cup of Assam
I became lost… dissolved in ritual…
Now
"Chado"…
The Way of Tea…has a whole new meaning to me
So much so…
The Leaf has become a sacred Tea House.
A place of mysticism and the…
Sweetness of your ceremony.

Manhatten Hat.

That hat I bought in Manhatten
Was like a friend to me
Eventually.

He kept me covered from the heavy heat
As that big old hot head sun's
Fire blazed like a gunfighter's roar.

Sheltered me from hail and rain
Like a minder always on call.

Always ready to keep me covered
When I needed protection
From the elements.

Hot or cold
Hung at the side of my head
Like he was hanging on the corner.
Killing time.

At home he would wait for me
By the door like a loyal pet.

Like a chauffer or a butler
Always ready to serve.
Dry or wet it didn't really matter
To my Manhatten straw hat.

He was always cool
Always indifferent
Always ready to face the weather.

Always at my disposal
What ever it was I'd ask
Like a long time acquaintance.
And he still is.

Blue Beat Heart.

I passed through your neighbourhood
And I was looking out for
I felt the Sun start coming through
Knew exactly what to do

Walking on the street you live
I had lots of Love to give
So I traveled deep into the past
To where the dice of Love where cast...

And then the music starts
Playing with the strings of my heart
And then the music starts
Playing with the strings of my heart

I passed through the old estate
In my mind I meditate
memories of you relate
To melodies in blue

In amongst the ruins
there's a melancholy tune
That tells an old-old story
Nothing very new

And then the music starts
Playing with the strings of my heart...

Eagle Eyes.

Eagle eyes rise above the cloudy skies
Far beyond the reason "Why?"
Where the fallen angels fly
Below the radar
Singing "Heayah - Heayah - Heayah !"

I need some altitude for altering my attitude
Vows continually renewed

I'm hovering in solitude
At times
Then the wind changes
And I rise, I climb.
Ascension !
Singing "Heayah - Heayah - Heayah !"

Eagle wings
Soar above all transient things.
So Eagle eagle eyes see only Heavenly bling.
Breath of Life caress the wind
This is how my people sing …
Singing "Heayah - Heayah - Heayah !"

Heart Headed.

Your consciousness is your Spiritual Heart
Faith in yourself is the first place to start.

I was born with my Head in my Heart
A disability or so it's been said.

My intellect decides through feeling
Judgement is suspended
Humility appealing.

To be secure within your own Love
To know you are Love
Is the only security that there is.

To let my empathy detox my Heart
Of all poisonous beliefes
That pollute my integral intention

To give Love
And enjoy Peace.

That is my Heart's most
Heady and truest release.

The Japanese Garden.

There's a Japanese Garden in Calderstones Park.
LeNoire used to call it the Beloved's Secret Garden
Or the Jazz Garden.
LeNoire liked Japanese gardens.
He also liked making analogies.
He like to point out the "Tauhid" in things.
There's a Unity in the apparant diversity" he'd say .
Or...
"It's like racou... Can you see ?"
        "It's like every mistake iz a new style" It's a
Ghanaian sayin… whirling Dervish'.
It's how master drummers, teach".
Djembé LeNoire had always admired the Japanese
sense of minimal maintenance.
The impression of random order...
The intuitive sense of composition
That arose, almost on it's own if given time.

The garden said it all for LeNoire.
He saw "The creation of a microcosm, or mini
landscape, based on an observation of the ordering
strategies of nature itself. A place to reinvent the
landscape of the mind.
Reality is focus" said LeNoire.

"And nature. Nature is the contrived accident.
I remember somebody tellin' me that all good ideas
are arrived at by accident... " Confided LeNoire. He
liked to ramble in a confidential manner.
"It's a Dervish thing... And a Jazz thang
Not an "Either- Or" thing But an "And-Also" thing
A sort of Zen thing I suppose".

LeNoire stared into deep space.
Momentarily pursueing a cross-cultural analogy.
The Japanese seem to take this as a rule of thumb
"Serendipity".   LeNoire liked the sound of that
word.

As synchronicity would have it, only that very
week
LeNoire had composed his very first Haiku
After several weak attempts.
This seemed like a perfect place to perform it.
The whole occasion had a sense of ritual about it.
Or so LeNoire had said.
Who knows. LeNoire had his reason's.
They weren't always that clear.
But more often than not they ended up making
sense eventually.
You just had to trust him.
Alli know is that today I feel like there's beauty in
everything" said LeNoire.
"And life... Life is precious. Ever so precious.
Like a precious stone hard but beautiful to behold".
I got a hint of where LeNoire was going with all
this.

He was resolving some plot or other.
He pointed to a rose.
"This..." said LeNoire "Is a symbol of the Glory of The Creator !"
I just looked. That much made sense.

A miniature waterfall
Characteristically named 'Cascade Mouth
'Taka Guchi' in Japanese.
And heralded by a stone lantern
That mimicked a tiny temple
Served as a place of offering.
And LeNoire offered up his Haiku
In much the same way you would a prayer.
As he spoke his voice condensed on contact with the cold Autumn air.
Peppermint breath risin' up like fresh incense as he recited:
"Oak trees sheddin' life
Granted by the hand of God
Acorns on the grass"
"The Cycle of Life and Death"
There was nothing more to be said.
As we left the garden LeNoire and myself watched the Autumnal sunshine spill gold across the lake.

We stood.
Looked
And were both lost momentarily
In the light of colours...
Original... Un-nameable...   And never to be seen again.

We felt privileged for being allowed to behold such
beauty.
Already he was wishin' that he'd brought a camera
to have captured the vision of splendour...
Even though he knew that film and chemicals
Could never have capture what he always
experienced
Walking in the Japanese garden.
Love's Walled Garden .
The Jazz garden.
        "Every mistake is a new style" said LeNoire...
"It's a Ghanaian sayin' you know...whirling...
Dervish.

Beach.

Always
Remembrance
Re-Collecting
Time
The mind's ebb and flow
Circular motion
Cyclic
Movement
Round the intimation of time
In rotation
each turn
in turn
a revolution

Petulant !
The swell of the sea

Scirocco like a two-tone suit
The billowing wind's
Impeccable roundness
curves the dunes

What it caused was a suspension
of suspicions
concerning Time

Perceptions
Our flawed awareness
It's eventual passing

At the centre a stillness
A knowing
A presence.

The Maritime pines Mambo
The forest flirts with the shore line
The Irish Sea's hand maiden
A beach blonde courtesan
In coral pink fronds
And knecklace of
Pale flesh coloured
scallop shells
tinged tangerine

Sequenced elegance
The shifting of the sea

Wave tips tinted saffron
By a chiffon sun.

Shimmying

an illusive motion
absent substance
Perceptible
the presence of light
Rolling
Rising
Undulating not unduly
Just shifting like the dunes
Encapsulating light in it's shadow

Bless My Cotton Blues.

Got a wild reputation / Got some descent alibis
Got an ear for a good story / Got a nose for people's
lies.
Got the light at the end / of a tunnel full of vision.
Got a wayward manner / Based on natural
intuition.

And I count my blessings with the Blues.
That the way I don't get confused...

Got my Blues harp / Got my prayer beads / Got my
pocket book of Wisdom.
Got my oral tradition / Got satirical derision.
Got my Frog songs / Got my poems / Got a special
way of knowing.
Got Angels surrounding me / When the baraka's
flowing.

And I count my blessings with the Blues.
That the way I don't get confused...

Blackbird.

After eulogizing as a Blackbird
My craft, troubadour inspired
Wolfshead sired
I realize I am actually out of the forest
And the silence at long last is everything
Truly it is all there is-
Truly everything.

Breath.

The Dervish Dances
In the garden of misplaced memorabilia
The halam-khat hollers
Down hollow avenues.

Begetter of backstreet backwater Blues
And battles that create the news
for this time this place this huddle...
These times of muddle.

The Gavelle unravels speech patterns that just
seem to happen.
Rhythms and scales for the Bluesman to wail
In tune with the hieght of the minaret
that sustains the flight of Bilal the Ethiopian
Muezzin's tale...

Following the truth of this life
Keeping the Truth in the light
Seeking the good in people

And praying that you're right...

We are breathing in and We are breathing out the one breath of the Universe. Something simple... Something fresh... Like a breath of Fresh air

Timeless tunes rise up from a pre-supposed past time
From times long past / Before time was prepacked
Yes! Your past and mine...
The Jazz Griot grins
knowing there is no beginning / No end
Only a circle that expands
A sacred hoop that hangs
on our limited understanding...
Of the ongoing present
The ever-present Now !

The Jelofo / the Jali / and the Jaré
Extemporaneously compose articles of Faith.
No time to waste no time to tarry
When there's so much need to communicate

The Delé juggles jurisdiscially.
Impongi puzzles ever so suspiciously...
For the need is greater than it's ever been
Where the grass is red no longer green
Carved in stone they killed the Dream
But Love'sTruth flows freely on Life's stream.

In a less complacent dimension Wird dancers awaken
Speaking' in broken trances

Of lost causes...

And Eternal romances...
A stray Word entrances !
A sly eye glances...
A forgotten alphabet reforms
A Lost tongue flexes regaining it's form...
&
As a Golden notion splinters into a Rainbow of infinite diversity

Steel tipped sonnets / Glass Oasis
Shaka's spear / Gazebo palm
Lion songs of Ancient Mali
Cowry shells / the hunter's charm
Café Bongo / Blue sarong
Chinese symbol / Indian Gong
Science Egyptian / Mohawk song
And a Sudanese zhikr that lasts hours long.

The Bass-line-lingo of the Sublinguistics
Sprouting green shoots that spring forth from a Medicine Beat / Blossoming into an opulent bouquet of opportunities for lots of Beautiful different thing's to say...

Each Word / Breathing' Life into Love
Huuuuuuuuuh !
Each breath of Love in turn becoming'...
Something' tangible.
Something' comparatively more real.
Something' quite substantial.
Credible enough for now / This moment.

Remembrance !
Trying not to loose sight of the higher ideal
Without which none of this is real
Without which real meaning evades us...

Remembrance... Each beath of love becoming
Simply becoming / merely becoming...

Something simple / Something Fresh
Like a breath of fresh air.

We are...

Breathing in and Breathing out
The One breath of the Universe.

Fish.

Brazilian Restaurant
Brazilian food
East Berlin.

Good.......
an unknown
fish/dish...

But you...
I'm not sure...

I thought I knew...
I thought you
understood...
I must'nt have...

or so it appears.

or so it appears...
in the paranoia
of others.

Breath Slowly.

Sometimes we consume time so fast
that we quickly forget
how
we may not have that much time left.

Other times we stop and take a breath .
Allah !
Flexing a free-flowing rhyme
Is like taking a deep breath with the mind...

We take in that which sustains our life force
and energizes our mind
As we exhale
Huu !
We loose the ties that bind

And there is a resuscitacion in the word-sound of
breath
Entwined with drumbeat and basslingual
rhythm...
Each life breath breathing life into a love
Beyond the will to possess.

Each breath of love something freely given
Something exhilarating

Something beautiful
Something deft.

Captain's Log.

Still adrift aboard this ship of fools, but…
I'm as alone within as ever- I was…
Silent, only the distant echo of the Montpelier
Codex
And the soothing strains of the Anonymous Blue
Ones
Troubadours of sorts-Sufi songs that sooth the
Soul
Soul torn to shreds by the desert wind
A breeze as subtle as the finest sand from Sahara…
I miss you !
Aye… miss, you!

I miss the life I once knew-
Sometimes
But I have no desire to pause and rewind-
I'm right at home in the present time-
The now frame of mind
And from the ashes of my yearning
A nothingness and an empty ache
A longing a sadness of heart
An inner poverty that waits
Just waits patiently…

As a mortal married to the machinations of
melancholy
And the pursuit of love at it's most Holy

"Holy art thou ! Oh Lord my God !
Blessed art thou and all that You decree !"
I surrender to the Silence within me
And the voice of the Lamb that told me to...
"Help them "
"But how ?" I ask-
"Just by being yourself !" the reply.

I am so full of blue emotion...
I could cry openly without shame.
I am crying deep down inside.
Silently-slowly consistently I weep
Way down deep within the recesses
Of my renunciative reclusive reveries
Waiting...

Cerebral Declutter.

I've been collecting
Too much other peoples stuff
Time to de-clutter
And call my own bluff.

Why waste time collating
Too much information
When a label is just
Another form of negation.

Of Life's ineffable
Infinate variations
On an ominous theme
Within the inconclusive

Timescape of a delusional dream.

Just some old school ideas
That need digesting
And reinterpreting
So they're more interesting.

Then abstract the wit from it
Season it and scatter
The ins and the outs of it
Until it doesn't really matter.

My responsibility is the ability
To respond and not just react
Despite the indeterminable facts
As long as it doesn't take too long
I suppose I can handle that.

Love's Vibration.

And then there was you.
The only vibration that was ringing true-
Loyal, over courteous, suppressed and blue.
The wind blew through the forest
That lay between us.
And a madman that none should trust...

Curtain.

I closed the curtain
But the light shone through
And when I looked
I saw there...

Only you.

The Declining Day.

By late afternoon the water has risen further.
I drift with the languid current.
The Irish sea now bronze and a shimmer of peuce
It's edge laced in salt-white and sun-scorched palm
leaves.

A powder blue sky so clear… So breathable.
As the winnowing wind's impeccable roundness
curves the dunes.
Carries me off into the glorious morning hour.
Seagulls circle in the distance.
The waves dance to a rhythm of their own.

Spherical the intimation of time, like the Earth.
A Circular motion / a cyclic movement like life.
Back to the beginning like the phases of the moon.
In rotation each turn, in turn an evolution of sorts
…

Sequenced elegance the shifting of the sea.
Wave tips tinted saffron by an orange chiffon sun.
The waves … and the water… rolling… rising…
Illusionary and surprising

There was a feather floating down, a piece of
down, fluffy, white.
Softer than snow, heavier than a cloud
A feather from the tail of a dove or the wing of an
Angel.

Either way a memento mori...
And a reason to be here now.

I look up at the sky... Smiling...
.
Off-white clouds display their silver-grey linings
A butter-milk sun shines through powder blue
A flock of terns heads off towards the horizon
Suddenly . Swift as a split decision
It evokes / a memory / a remembrance of you.

Out at sea the depths seethe as the sea breathes
The sea speaks / the sea thinks
The boat creaks / the sea links
A myriad tributaries that feed into the warm bloodstream
Of this now-tropical place / Trace it's trajectory
Back to the ocean from whence it came...

Absent substance yet...
Perceptible the presence of light beneath the water.
Shimmying an illusive motion.
As a school of blue dolphins lead me back to the land.
The Light is !
All colours and no colour !

Trust in Love.

Let it all go – bro...
Breathe more deeply

And lean a little harder
On the staff of your Faith
Then …wait…you'll see
An apparition of a brighter
Newer possibility-
Breath- Breath some more-
Let time pass-Trust in your destination-
Relax you are traveling too fast-
Let time pass-
You can't out pace
The present moment
Let go of the past- So what is possible
Can emerge-Trust in your own worth
Trust in the best that you deserve-
Breathe deeply and Trust in the Beloved
Breathe deeply-Let go and learn to trust yourself-
Trust in your own Love.

The Now.

Sweet Non-Existance / Radiant Night
Luminous darkness / like a Sea of Black Light
Womb of the Formless / outside of Time
Perpetual Presence / the Slayer of Mind...

Right Now ! Here in the Now
Right Now ! Right Here in the Now...
Here in the Ever Present moment
Here in the Ever Present Now...
The Ever Present Now !

Observe only causes / Life's rippling effects

Golden with Silence / The Tranquil depths
Peace is of Being / The end of all pain /
Shapeless and Colourless / No loss No gain ...

Right Now ! Here in the Now
Right Now ! Right Here in the Now...
Here in the Ever Present moment
Here in the Ever Present Now...
The Ever Present Now !

Hadramaut.

With it's theme park curls
And Disney Pearls
We've created a corpse
Wearing make-up

We'll compete for it's bones
With dog-like tones
Till the day that the dead
Start to wake up

Just a few short note from the Hadramaut
Just some memories I hold to dispell my doubts
Mama said let that boy boogie
It's in him and it's gotta come out

Woeful in worship
And weeping in streams
We chant in our waking
We sing in our dreams

The humbler the sinner

The surer he'll find
A heart that's been broken
When polished still shines

Jazzoetry.

A rainbow trout of imagination
Is
The activity
of
The Soul
Leaping waterfalls
of
Creature energy
and
Creative essence
to the summit of
Opulent articulation.

The reverie of linguistic linguini.

Consommé of the consummate connoisseur.

Improvised oratory devices
mixed with fire and ice
And measured
by
Murtajal

Darkness and Light
in
Instigation.

Jazz is unlimited variations
Endless combinations.

Dervish Pen.

With pen and ink, that's how I think.
With words on the page, I set the stage.
With the Beloved in mind, my thoughts unwind.
Open your heart. See what you find.
An endless sea of space and time !
Where planets spin, and novas shine.
Whats mine is yours. What your is mine .
The Mercy of The One Divine .

I know it's in your Heart / But my Mind Forgets
I'll try and write it all down step by step Beloved.

With melody I set words free.
With breath of life I add the spice.
With tone of soul I take control.
Of rhythm's rock, and thunder's roll .
From harmony of rhythm flows,
The sound of things too vast to know.
Stars in the sky that softly glow.
Darkness to light is how we grow.

I know it's in your Heart / But my Mind Forgets
I'll try and write it all down step by step Beloved.

Desert Sky.

The stars shone bright in the desert sky

I was laying kinda low / But feeling high
Like an ancient Moor amidst the dunes
On a magic carpet digging Ancient tunes.

Sandalwood insence / A silken sari
Promises tasting of Turkish delight
A silver necklace / A green satin cushion
Allah reveals wonders on into the night.

Like the crystal streams/ Kool & free
I'll Remember you / Remember Me
Like the wind in the trees/ Kool & free
I'll Remember you / Remember Me
The fish in the sea / Kool & Free
I'll Remember you / Remember Me
The Birds & Bees / Kool & free
I'll Remember you / Remember Me
I'll Remember you / Remember Me
I'll Remember you / Remember Me
Remember you / Remember Me
Remember you / Remember Me
I'll Remember you / Kool & Free !

Midnight opened up the sky
Like a jewel studded casket
Emerald eyes sparkled like
Some Oriental magic
Mysterious gems with that which mends
engraved in every facet.
Thoughts drifted to that special One
Whose memory they crafted.

Like the crystal streams/ Kool & free

I'll remember you / Remember Me
Like the wind in the trees/ Kool & free
I'll remember you / Remember Me
The fish in the sea / Kool & Free
I'll remember you / Remember Me
I'll Remember you / Remember Me
I'll Remember you / Remember Me
I'll Remember you / Remember Me
I'll Remember you / Kool & Free !

Spades in Shades.

Spades in Shades. Cultural detective. Culturally diverse.
Free association. Free verse.
Sun-glasses / night-time / we're in doors.
Sub-cultural. "Kool ! Kool !".

Cynical " trying to conceal identity". More observant; "I'd recognise him even with shades on !"

Let me explain something..... Visually Impaired Artist formerly known as
"Baby you know AAH AAH I luvvs yah ! But No ! Then Who in heck is this ?"

Spades in Shades. Mmmmmmmm ! Sounds like a Negro name. Kinda Bluesy like ... familiar". Spades in Space, more like / conceal red eyes.
Others missing the cultural gags. Where I'm coming from.

Just stuck on the word "Identity". Cos it's such a mysterious word. All of a Sudden .

Anthropologists'll be thinking "OK! OK ! It's a Black thing".
But actually it's a bit, more than just a Black thing.
Family lineage. Uncles & Aunties. Races & Religions. God rest their Souls !
Wait for it !   The Black & White Mistrel Show.
Wait for it ! Fully extended family scenario. Country cousins. In laws & out laws.

There's a lot of mixed race people in Liverpool. People with names like Iqbal MacTavish, Soraya O'Shaughnessy, Jimbo Gadaffi, Ram-Jam Butty, Sinbad O'Toole...
To name but a few.

People who eat Mad-Ras curried Scouse, Lancashire hot and sour, Ishmails halal burgers, and Chippatti chip-butties. It does peoples heads in. But some people are nutty.

As they used to say down Scotty Road, "Mommas baby! Poppas maybe?"

Courtesy of the merchant navy. We're all related to someone shady.
And The Way is merciful and sides with the needy.

Culturally diverse "Cultural detective". I think I better dance now. That's a street directive.

(Beatbox into Slavepool).

The Beloved Only.

I'm not doing this for creed, class, race, style,
fashion, taste, LFC, you or me,
the hienous calumny of high-treason, or any other
particularly superficial sectarian reason.

I'm doing this for the Beloved ! Just for the Beloved !
And the Beloved only ! And I'm not lonely.

I'm not doing it so people like me
I'm not doing it so people'll think I'm Hip or that
I'm particularly I'm devout.
Ask me what I think about what people think and
I'll tell you without a doubt, in good clear English
"Nowt.
Even though I know there's a lot of ignorance out
there round and about of which I'm sure your all so
aware. I really don't care. So there !

I'm doing this for the Beloved ! Just for the Beloved !
And the Beloved only! And I'm not lonely.

I'm not doing this because I like letting it all hang
out on stage.
Or because I'm secretly nursing a brooding rage.
For vengeance earns a bitter wage For those who
rattle history's cage.

I'm doing this for the Beloved ! Just for the Beloved !
And the Beloved only! And I'm not lonely.

I do this not because I have the aspirations of a sage
that painstakingly peruses the revealed page, for
comfort as I near old age the pace of which is hard
to gauge.

I'm doing this for the Beloved ! Just for the Beloved !
And the Beloved only ! And I'm not lonely.

I do this not for the vain perspicacity of applause
Or argue what's rightfully mine or wrongfully
yours.
Or cut the Oneness into shapes where man's ego
subverts Agape
With curl of lip and churlish jape, and jibe that
talks of place and tribe.
And cheesy lies that deny fate when none can tell
their sell by date.
Or tell if Paradise awaits.

I'm doing this for the Beloved ! Just for the Beloved !
And the Beloved only ! And I'm not lonely.

I do this not to thumb my nose at them and those
Who due to the pointless poise of their
postmodernist simulacrity
And the opaque nature of their omnique-clarity
And it's vacuous lack of conviction.
Can't tell the funk from the fiction. No !

I'm doing this for the Beloved ! Just for the
Beloved !
And the Beloved only ! And I'm not lonely.

I do this for Peace ! Mercy ! Grace !
Truth -Light -The Living and The Good
And all the Most Beautiful Names of God
That descend from sweet Heaven above
For we the people of Clay and Mud.

I'm doing this for the Beloved ! Just for the Beloved !
And the Beloved only ! And I'm not lonely. Honest !

Geopolitico.

A body half clothed in rags drags at the current.
The river half concealing it... half notices / it's
weight.
A life form rotting away / Sways.
The day / The date ... Both too late.

This macabre disarray is it social decay ?
Or one of the more destructive quirks of how
power-tricks
work their narrow wisdom into a Tribalism !
I apologise I meant the professorial expertise
of governmental visionaries that forever tease
like the sickly-sweet scent of putrifying flesh.

But when the Truth seems unwise.
Euphemisms tend to, ever so endearingly,
patronise.
Call it the orthodoxy of official lies.
Or just murder in disguise.
Even curiosity hides it's well meaning liberal eyes.

Time dictates the facts / As the media fakes outrage
To our will to sit back / and watch Life as a stage.
And with each passing day as more lives slip away
Know ye well that Death lurks where the powerful shirk.
Once we add the equation
War equals Weapons equals Arms deals equals Work.

From passive resistance to open aggression
Oppression is the death of Freedom expression.
And in England Rain falls softly
Quiet tears shed for rose petals on a flower bed.
And a poem... Carved into the Earth's bones

Smoke.

Dust to dust and in between we dream
if we are fortunate enough to find rest.

In my Dreamwalking I smoke the Peace pipe
with the holyghosts of my ancestors
watching the smoke rise up on the voices of the wind.

Four rivers meet in me and ring bell like
as they sing the flesh of my humanity
from the bare bones of my ignorance.

I reinvent my essential self
in the sacred manner...

In an effort to once again become
Someone I can live with...

Someone closer to The Source...

Closer to ...
The Giver of Colours
and
The Bestower of Form...

Closer to You than I am now...

The Didgeri Dunes.

Communicating through life
Without the use of cellular fones
We collect shells and fircones
Sketching out our demarcation zones.

Clambering clumsily up the side of the Didgeri
dunes
We wax and wane with the wind
To maintain our balance

And in the dunescape of our middle ground
We take a look around and settle down ...to
sharing.

Earth walking we leave the sea and head for the
trees
Where I dance with the Standing People
For the forest is my patch. It is here I feel equal.

In my hands some small golden fir-cones

Gifts from the dancing pines
My pockets are full of sea-shells
Wrapped in the sands of time...

The suave pink sun light breaks through the
dancing tree-tops...
Firing it's golden shafts of light like arrows
Deep into the heart of the forest
Sheltering amidst Summer light hadows...
We stop to bask..
And where Sun-light kisses Earth much healing
takes place...
So it is with us.
So it is with us.

Possibility.

You want to write a Love poem
Pick up the pen then
But first consider...
The possibilities of confrontation.
The confrontation of possibility.

Look at the page...
You are that page.
The page is...

Something upon which you can project yourself.
A feel / a state of mind / a field of energy.
A construct or a manifestation of self.

The empty page
A place where a transference of impulses

Continually takes place...

Love is the confrontation of possibility.
The possibilities of confrontation.

Pick up the pen
Go 'ed if you think it's that easy.
But first consider...

A Barbados Moment.

The palm trees in Barbados
Swayed like Samba dancers
In the cozy Caribbean breeze.
Their frayed serated leaves
Like a Steel pan man's frilly sleaves.
Maracas, bongos, cabasas, congas
Co-co nuts, mangos, and purple passion fruits
Palm trees like Calypsonians
In exotic carnival suits
Limbo dancing in the hot Bajan wind
As you perused inside the antique shack
I stayed outside and grinned.

Devastating.

Hold love in your heart too tightly
It will harden into stone
Only when that heart is broken
Is the Inner beauty known

Devastating and alluring
Drink this cup I call my heart

How could I ignore your calling
Love is where all journeys start.

Precious gems memento-moris
Reason still to be here now
Love's humility most gory
Lover wherefore art thou now.

Devastating and alluring
Drink this chalice from my heart
How could I ignore your calling
Love is where all journeys start.

Dew-drops drip
From sanguine petals
Rosebud lips and eyes of glee
Guile to test Sir Gawain's mettle
Damsel dark come joust with me.

Devastating and alluring
Drink this Grail within my heart
How could I resist your calling
Love is where all journeys start.

Dream Walking.

My shadow sleeps.
I surrender myself to he Great Mystery
In the sacred manner...
For there is much that I do not know
I push my fingers into my chest and
I open up the contents of my Heart
letting it 's seething mess of blood

soaked scar-tissue bleed it's seering
flow into my open contorting consciousness

It is here that I wrestle
with the various forms
of internalised terrorism
Obese insecurities that threaten to engulf me
dulling my eye, strangling my tongue
devouring my sanity
and my lust for life

It is here that I struggle
towards the Dimness of the Light of a clearer
insight
into my own Right & Wrong...

I hurt, I cry, I grow strong
When we cry we pray
And our Tears Purify and decorate
Our prayers with sincerity
Each word seasoned with the Hearts True Essence
This is what makes your Love so precious

As I journey closer to The Source...
Closer to The Giver of Colours
The Bestower of Form...
The Nourisher / The Sustainer.

Closer to Home
Closer to the Lover of The Two Easts and The Two
Wests
Who requires no slumber or the need for rest
Who knows Who We were before we were who we

are
And Who sets each individual their own personal test.
Their own Perfect test.

Dust to dust and in between we dream.
If we are fortunate enough.

Drifting.

Yeah! I be just drifting and this is how it go ...

Just moving with the flow
Cos that's the only way I know
Like everything that grows
I though by now you'd know.

Taste the Truth of Peace
Waters pure and sweet
No need to compete
Because everythings complete.

Just drifting just drifting
High planes drifting
Paradigm Shifting.

High up in sky
Where the eagles fly
Clouds just pass me by
Sunshine in their eyes

Let your Soul aspire
Hear celestial choirs
Concentrate your dreams

Feel what freedom means.

Just drifting just drifting
High planes drifting
Paradigm Shifting.

Earthwalking.

Semi-contemptuous of my clowning
You stand silent / rooted like the Pine...
Your eyes closed...facing that which is beyond .
As I contemplate you / You shine !

I hear you listening to the seas eternal rhythm.
You open your eyes like an answers been given
Heading off towards the sky-line and the sea
As sudden and as swift as a split decision.

Walking North along the beach I leave you and the
sea to talk
And in my Soul searchings I practise the Medicine
song.
And as always I walk.
The day is short but the beach is long.

Yin and Yang.

A warm red sun
And
A cool green moon
That's
My Yin and Yang
Complimentary cartoons.

Hood Bluze.

It was dark times.
The Hood lay across my shoulders at first.
A fashion statement.
Then I noticed it in the mirror. I pulled it over my head.
And I noticed him observing me. Self-scrutiny.
Scratching the surface of the face
With the eyes of a traveler A gypsy. A Nomad.

Watching, monitoring. The World, people, me .
Looking for hidden meaning. The truest stories, the best stories. The Ancient story. The One story. The Only story.

Hating me at times. The look in his slow brooding eyes.
Pain glowing darkest bright.
Features shaded by the black hood of his sweat-suit top
rising up from inside the upturned pointed collar of a black leather jacket.

Dread Robin. Robin of the Hood.
Knowledge of self a rose, a precious stone.

Cold eyes over my shoulder scolding with their heated gaze.
Sneering at my naiveté, my stupidity, openness.
Ignorance the true shackles of my serfdom.
Running with the wind. Drinking in the freshness of the rain.

The teachings tell us that our best friend and our worst enemy both dwell within us.
Mine dwells at my right hand shoulder. A chip off the old block.
Carved into a new environment.

A panther at home amidst the dark shadows of the greenwood.
Integrated. An organic creature.
Complex and distinctive in it's:
Language spoken;
Rituals performed;
Manifestation of the survival instinct;
Raw expressions of Life's essence.

And this time. This is a ritual time.

We are stories made from stories. The act of speech. Us telling stories to ourselves. About ourselves. About who we are. Naming ourselves.
Brothers and Sisters !

Sounds emanate from the shadow world.
This is how we speak ourselves into existence.
This is why we rap.
Orature-Orality-ID-Reality.
Orature: a Time based Ritual.
A ritual time.
Identity a regenerated living enactment of memory.
Incomplete erasures still resonating.
Ancestral Echoes. Shadows in the forest.

Orality a way of perceiving time.

Voice ebullient. He preached to me.
The bass-line lingo of the sublinguistics.
Mouth invisible. Mouse invincible.
Sipped sweet tea as he delicately dipped his arrows in it's venom.

Hidden in the darkness of the black hood pulled over his head. He spoke from within the shadow of veiled knowledge. In a disenfranchised tongue wet with savouring the concentrated taste of strategic flavours.
"Mmmm... and the Blues is a form of Dervish-hood", he croons.

"This is how we empower ourselves as individuals and as groups. As humans. He emphasized a prayer from a book of sacred rhymes. The power of Black-chat. Is the power of backchat. The power of the word.

Life-histories evolved from a rhythm different from those regulated by their symbiosis with the central placenta.
The absent centre.

Truth versus 'Reale Politique'". Hood sneers.
Watches me.
Black invisibility and Namelessness.
Studies. Assesses.
Guards psychological territory.
Pantherhood producing meaningful shapes

amidst the abstract palimpsests of systematic negation, omission, misrecognition and inappropriate definitions of the other.
My Sisters and Brothers!

Reality is a time based art.
Like Dread Robin of The Hood.
Peace an indeterminate entity.
Solidarity, unstable in all it's aspects.
A Living narrative. Liquid. Flowing. Fluid.
That's what we came from.
That's how we Human Beings do it.

A story to be sung. Our culture.
A Something spoken. Not found.
Sculptured Soul welded from retold histories.
Unsolved mysteries located in the future.
Flickering lights and dancing shadows.
In the forest darkness.
Our Inner-Heartness.
Our Natural Good.
"This is a ritual time"
"We are a ritual people "says The Hood.

He is watching.
Face hidden he lingers at my right-hand side.
Holding my sword arm.
Drawing me near he whispers...
"The eloquence of sublimated fire-terrain".
Murmurs the mantra of unarticulated fears.
Historical experiences. Lost traditions.
Spoken in forbidden tongues.

The very sounds of which challenge.
The assumed authenticity.
Of any sense of mastery.

He points to a fire in the library !
As real as the night is black. As clear as the night is fact.
A beacon !
Light !
Focus !
And the emergence of detail as the shadow shifts.
Moves across the face chased by a glowing radiance.
Inner Guidance. The Dance of Khidr. A dance of Light.

I face the mirror and pull the black hood back to reveal ...
A pleasant insight.
Not the Grim Reaper ! Not Death !
Nothing that they may have left ...
But Life !
Focused life.
And a Dance of Light !

And each of us merely words in progress. Each of us a part of the Neighbourhood in process. The Hood in Jazz-chord progression. No more . No less. It's all part of life's test. There's no worse. No best. And so after the Truth, then what is there left ?

A name, a rose by any other.

The Edge of Dawn.

At the edge of dawn light ascends upwards from
the heavens
Salmon pink day-light kisses the sky…
Breathes life into the blue beyond.

Waves of rolling lines lead to the curved edge of the
horizon
Curved beyond our natural vision
Part of the overall roundness of this place, now.
Since the water has risen.

Beneath the waves a rusty sign that reads
Merseyrail
Black and white barriers separate road from trail.
A chocolate box assortment of shops
A chippy / an off license / a bright red pillar box
Covered in barnacle spots…
Then the sunken road drops off.

I pull in my oars and float
An owl peering over the side of my aqua-marine
boat…
Beneath me an aquatic park flanked by houses
Angular shapes softened by curves in places.
Brash red-brick façades sweetened by
Pink pastel shades in plaster.

Grander designs in sobering sandstone ,
Gold domed with wrought iron spires,
Now nestled amidst mottled green

Flickering like ceramic fixtures
In Mother Nature's gold fish bowl.

I lean over and run my hand through the walm water.
Green soothes as the light moves through blue bell glades
Colonnades of Romanesque stature swaying like sea-weed
Beneath the glittering waves ... that sing ...
Of the water's ebb and flow, a remembrance of time's past.

Spectral my presence as I drift above the foamy sway.
But by now I'm used to this...
At the centre of the moment the horizon beckons...
Infinite to the eye but ever calling.
Compelling, cajoling, coaxing the gaze outwardly.

I ghost past the tip of what was once a triumphant tower
Hung with storm lanterns like a harbour bouy.
Using the submerged road below me as my salty old sat-nav.
Red tarmac speckled with grey and white gravel.
It is here the marinading metropolis stops.
Red turns to beige / Road to sand
And all fade from my view
As if they alone knew my true destination.

Where the wind blows, and the water flows free.

At the centre of all reason there is a sense of light
At the edge of that light the water waits for us…
A transcendent order beyond the chaos.

Slavepool.

A seaport sprang from the blood of slaves
In the pool of Life a macabre parade
Human marketplace Black flesh for trade
I'm talking African people held in chains.

Cargo bought and sold on the cotton exchange
With the gum and the rum and the sugar cane
Branded like beasts who feel no pain
And all for Merrye Olde Englande's gain.

But things are changing, rearranging
Cos only We can clear our name.
Growing, knowing, tradewinds are blowing
Adhaan is flowing / Faces are glowing
Reciting the most Beautiful names.

The Slaves of Allah are praying again.
Reclaiming their names / Staking their claims.
Things'll nevva be the same.

Pirates auctioned and pitched / Parliament pitted
their wits

The church & the mosque sold out our soul for gold
That's how come those cats got rich
With the capital they carved a cosy niche
For the cotton industry and the nouveau riche.

Excuse me I don't mean to preach
But Black blood sweat and tears
Toiled and slaved for years
To create all the wealth interest free
Banking, shipping, industry.

Black poverty paved the way to prosperity
John Bull cashed in on our posterity.
Legitimised robbery of Afrikan property
And an Islamic legacy buried in history.

But history changing, rearranging
Cos only We can clear our name
Growing, knowing, tradewinds are blowing
Adhaan is flowing / Faces are glowing
Reciting the most Beautiful names.

The Slaves of Allah are praying again.
Reclaiming their names / Staking their claims.
Things'll nevva be the same.

Our real contribution dismissed and forgotten
By delusions of grandeur corrupted and rotten.

Slave ship to the cotton picking slave plantation
Sold down the Swannee to dehumanisation.
Jump down turn around pick a bail of nuthin'
But a bullwhip noose, or a gun or somthin'.

Imports exports holiday resorts
The imput was largely ours of course.
The worlds largest ever unpaid workforce
With the most abundant source of natural
resources
And we didn't profit one iota more is the worse.

Our mineral rich land, time, energy, and pain
Help to build an Empire that ruled in shame.
Now dismissed go collective claims for credit
Or a share in the wealth of that direct debit.

Just 400 years of shackles and chains
Attitudes, slander, media campaigns
Outrageous claims that retard our aims
By the trivialisation of Race Hate games.

But People changing, rearranging
Cos only We can clear our name
Growing, knowing, tradewinds are blowing
Adhaan is flowing / Faces are glowing
Reciting the most Beautiful names.

The Slaves of Allah are praying again.
Reclaiming their names / Staking their claims.
Things'll nevva be the same.

If you've evva been on the dole or without a home
you'll realise what I'm saying that it all began
By a way of life that's carried on
By keeping innocent people down.

Liverpool !
City in a society built on a truth that's cruel
Once upon a time you were the nation's jewel
Now discarded like a worn out industrial tool
With redundant rhetoric and bourgeois rules.

Northern Workers used and abused like the Slaves
of old
That's how the Beatles got their Blues music down
cold
Cos they were born from a Black man's Soul.
That's why most folks understand. And I guess
that's kool
So let the song remain the same, Slavepool !
And The Blues speaks Truth and Guides to The
Right Way.
And The Blues speaks only Truth and guides to The

Straight Path.

Ya-yo ebina osé!
Ya-yo-lay ebina osé!
Ya-yo ebina osé!
Ya-yo-lay ebina osé!
Ya-yo la!
Kundo pa!
Ya-yo tuffu!
Kedjayii!
Kundo pa kokuloko!
Waba nulé desoloko!

(Dedicated to Delado: School of Africa, and the Class of '81. Bless.)

The Sistahs.

You held council with The Hi-Rise Sisterhood
And at least one of them said that I was no good.
But of course I knew at least one of them would.
Par for the course. So it's understood

The Way It Is Blues.

If your baby left you / In the pouring rain.
And she went to London / By a coach not a train..
And you find yourself thinking of what you can do
And those Blues start a creeping/ All up around you.

You gorra face it kid that's just the way it is !
Hmmm-Hmmm-Mmmm...Hmmm-Hmmm-
Mmmm...
You gorra face it kid that's just the way it is !
Hmmm-Hmmm-Mmmm...Hmmm-Hmmm-
Mmmm...

You might hate her ideas/ She might laugh in your
face
She might batter your ears / Cos she don't like your
taste.
She might juggle your words / And confuse what
you say.
It might not figure right / But just leave it that way.

You gorra face it kid that's just the way it is !
Hmmm-Hmmm-Mmmm...Hmmm-Hmmm-
Mmmm...
You gorra face it kid that's just the way it is !
Hmmm-Hmmm-Mmmm...Hmmm-Hmmm-
Mmmm...

I may act like a monkey/ But I sure aint no ape.
If I give you my heart / Don't pull it out of shape.
When my feelings are tender / And I'm lonesome
and blue.
I'll write return to sender / from me back to you .

You gorra face it kid that's just the way it is !
Hmmm-Hmmm-Mmmm...Hmmm-Hmmm-
Mmmm...

Mutha Songs.

Me Mutha used to Sing me Freedom Songs
Now I've grown I've figured out the Reason.
That's the way the woman stayed Strong.
All things in due Season.

Me Mutha used her songs to revitalise all our hopes
They helped us realise our dreams
As she explored her own ability
to cope and plan and scheme.

Burning illusions/ Makings sense of the confusion
That's how she taught me to live my life.
Me Mutha's Songs were always Rooted
In The Ancient and Wise.

Me Mutha's songs' were for the child.
That would be denied because its skin-tone's rare
Or its tongue deemed too common.
May Me Mutha's songs' keep that child
From stealing and robbing.

And street violence/ cops/ thugs and phony-ass people.
The dole / the system/ and drugs that are lethal.

Leaching/ lynching/ witch-hunting and bitching.
Cracked headed kids trigger fingers itching.

Yeah ! When me mutha sang it was more than a song
It was a way of showing me the right from the

wrong.

Me Mutha used to Sing me Freedom Songs
Now I've grown I've figured out the Reason.
That's the way the woman stayed Strong.
All things in due Season.

Me Mutha's songs' laughed and Me Mutha's Songs
cried.
Lorrrrrrd ! How Me Mutha's Songs cried
For all the lost lives/ And how quick time flys.

And everytime I lift the veil from my eyes
I see her sing the Blues. The Boogy. Be-Bop and Jive.
I remember when she was still alive
How the songs brought tears to her jitterbugging
eyes.

Me Mutha's Songs helped me to survive.
From Way-way back when I was a child.
Running wild ! Hell Yeaah ! Wild & Free !
Climbing fire escapes/ or high up into a tree
Anywhere/ any place high enough to see.

The visions that me Mutha showed me.
Climbing in bombed out buildings
Up onto derilict rooves.
Climbing hills and mountains.
Scatting on a groove.

Me Mutha's Songs were the sounds of suppressed
realities.
Mixed marriages and one parent families.
That's why I'm burning false history and writing

the sequal.
Using pen & paper to relate to people.

Me Mutha used to Sing me Freedom Songs
Now I've grown I've figured out the Reason.
That's the way the woman stayed Strong.
All things in due Season.

I Know That.

Sitting here on lonely afternoon
Wondering if things will work out right real soon
Adding up al my reasons left to care
Feeling like I've had more than my fair share
Honing my patience like a precious blade
Remembering Texas and those Golden days
With Joy in my heart I'll find a better way

And I know that God likes laughin'
Cos I saw it in a dream
I was clowning / He was smilin'
And He sanctioned it as clean
And I know that God likes Humans
Cos He told me to be me
Cos he wants us to be happy
And He wants us to be free...

In my heart I wear my dancing shoes
As I count my blessings with the Blues
Cos I know God always leaves us clues
In every Soul a precious jewel

Distill my patience through my pen

I'll walk through fire to write again
I'll dance like Kelly in the rain
And whirl till God Alone's to blame

And I know that God likes dancin'
Cos I saw it in a dream
See I rocked in thaub and turban
And He told me it looked mean
And I know that God likes Humans
Cos He told me to be me
Cos He wants us to happy
And He wants us to be free.

Haiku #4.

Raindrops tap dancing

Summer drizzle on a hot tin-roof

An aloof muse.

March 3rd 1993.
(Gladys Mary Coles Workshop John Moores Ba Hons)

It was like the first day
of April
today.

Spring
at
the beginnng

of February

I search the ground for primroses.

Why not ?
I mean everything else
is changing....

So why not the seasons.

Mother nature
was never known to follow
man's reason.

Early morning
sunlight
a new day
an insight.

Indian Shoes.

Eyes
Full of sighs
Mouth
Full of fruit
Prayed
Like a song
Sang
Like a lute.

Sad
Soul seething
Heart
Steeped in pain

Woke-up
From dreaming
Calling-out
Your name...

Everyones got Opinions
Everyone shares Views

They say ;
"Nevva judge an Indian...
Untill you've walked
In his shoes"

Browsed
Beneath the bric-a-brac
Disturbed
A lorra mice
Sorted-out
All of the loose talk
Dried-out
My eyes

There's
Only One direction
Whatever
Way you choose
Even
If your wide-eyed
You
Just might miss the clues...

Everyones got Opinions
Everyone shares Views

They say ;
"Nevva judge an Indian...
Untill you've walked
In his shoes"

We Rollin'.

Creating my own harmony
From somewhere deep within
Feel my Spirit rising
And that's when the Vibes begin.

I feel my heart pulsating
It's the kick drum of the Soul
In silent meditation
I adjust the controls.

And that's how we roll
Yeah ! This is how we roll
And we rollin'
And we Rrroooollin'
We rollin' in Love...

Sometimes it's your smile
Sometimes it's your sweet eyes
Sometimes it's your magic
Sometimes it's... I just don't know why.

Rrroooollin'
We roolin' on we rollin' on
We rollin' on down the road.

Griot FM.

Silence Sound Opposites Abound
Rhythm Functions Inbewteen
Syncopates the Middle Ground.

From the Wisdom of the Ancients too vast to mention
With humility we target our truest intentions
Sound's strategic essentials sketched in pencil
For mapping the self and it's inner dimensions.

Silence Sound Opposites Abound
Rhythm Functions Inbewteen
Syncopates the Middle Ground.

May this Earth-Jam Session regulate the Soul
May these Griot harmonies help to blend
May the Will of the Universe be in control
And may my words shine with the light of the Friend.

Silence Sound Opposites Abound
Rhythm Functions Inbewteen
Syncopates the Middle Ground.

Urban Mango Rituals.

I'm reading James Baldwin's "Another Country".
A close friend sits opposite me she also has a copy...
Which I bought for her, btw, from Atticus, a
second hand book shop.
It has a nice cover very 'Beat'.

In her copy a line has been hi-lighted on page
seven...
By a previous owner. She reads it to me...
Baldwin's omniscient narrator speaks:
" A Nigger, said his father, lives his whole life, lives
and dies to a beat".

We sit and we read occasionally exchanging
sometimes furtive,
Sometimes knowing glances.
We taste the coffee... Swelter in the mid-afternoon
heat.
Sierra Maestra workshop Manteca in the back
ground
From a session I taped in the ballroom of the
Hardman Hotel last year.

The seasons have come 'round again.
I hear myself play bongo's through the speakers
When I play it to El Gringo he will swear it is him.
Out the window L8... Feels/Looks like Baldwin's
Harlem & Greenwich Village all rolled into one...
And the Beat Goes On !

New Designs Realigned with an Ancient Time
When we lived with the land and the living was
fine.
Sweet like mango. Hot like chillie.
Like a solid vibration rooted in Unity
With the thick green seldom seen undergrowth
That Sprawls as it Crawls across the ground.
Like a sound Heey ! Yeeah !

I'm singing in my comic-sleazy Dean Martin voice
"Summertime and the living is easy
Fish are jumping and the cotton is high
Your daddies rich and yo' momma's good lookin'
So hush little baby don't you cry..."
At the helicopter hovering in the sky'

It's Summertime in Liverpool town
The air is full of African sounds
Sonic vibes rooted in Unity with
the thick green Seldom seen undergrowth
the Sprawls as it Crawls across the ground
Of the South End of this City.

Bodacious brass solidifies like lava
Into a tree of sound whose roots
Spread like forbidden knowledge
Across the sweat drenched dancefloor...
Upwards through the forest of legs
That tremble with the rumble of bass.
The unstoppable movement of a
Thunder that combines Power with Grace.

In pubs and bars, clubs and cars...
house's flats and tenement yards
it's carried on the wind like a leaf or a spark
Yeah! Especially downtown
After Sundown... Yeah! After dark.

Heart beats pound as the air resounds
with rhythms from the Earthy ground
Feelings over-run their bounds
And...I feeel Good! Ooowwoh Wooowooo!
I knew that I would...
And the Beat Goes On!

Clubland populated with copulating wild life
In the half-lit moonlight.
This is the nightlife
Milky   White-Cream   coloured-Beige-Chocolate-
Spray Tanned
Bronzed-Red- Yellow-Brown and Black bodies
caught up
In the hot tomali beat...

Feelings flowing like the fever that feeds the frenzy
of the Flavella.
As mysterious as the curiously seductive Kasbah
As dangerous as the compulsively calling Ghetto...
Liverpool Echo! Echo! Echo!

In Sefton Park the Last Tango leaving some lovers
Frothing-fumbling-falling to the soft mossy floor
To wind some more/ And some more /And some
more

And some more babyyyy!

Red veined bodies entwine like mixed bloodlines
Clinging like the vines that find their way across
Centuries and Oceans...
Around the rabbit warren of city streets
And their wall to wall alehouses
Down the alleyways
Up seething stairwells
And into people's lives.

Grapevines and hybrid blood lines
That bind as they wind their way
Through wires and circuits and the
Moist-fresh hot-wet close-cut atmosphere...

Fuelled by the Souls that once filled
Once upon time clubs like the Ibo, Yoruba, Calabar,
Sierre Leone, West Indian,
Fat Johnnies, Dutch Eddies, Casablanca, Jamaica
House, Caribbean Centre, Somali Club, Sudanese
Silver Sands, Malay Hollywood, Yemeni Al
Haram, All Nations, The International, Zanzibar,
Timepiece, Pun and Babalou
And many other places old and new
Where we did what we did / As we used to do how
we do.

Neighbourhood hang outs
Where the sound of the jungle meets the beat from
the street.
Homeboys hanging around pool-tables
We bathed in the heat of the mango-fresh

Mambo-Reggae-Samba-Motown-Hi-Life-Blue
Beat-Cha-Cha
The handclap, the thigh slap, the drum and the
boogaloo foot tap.
We be...We be...We be...
More than just music
More than just dance
More than just Heartbeats
Pulsating like the hot salsa sound of Al Barrio
Writhing in a passionate embrace that echoes
The Love that is the Life of the Inner City peoples
in full flow.

We be the Music
That is the food of Lovers of the Human Soul
Performers with a spicey social role
Shimmy a shim as you sample the fried squid at
Sunnyland Slims...
Taste a Mexican taco at El Macho's...
Black pepper fried chicken at the Sierre Leone
Red Beans & Rice very nice with Caribbean spices.
Hot Pepper Sauce puts the fire in el Corezone.

Music pumping like a Mardi Gras in season
Cooking like a Carnival outa control
Cowbells dancing, and imploding
Timbales exploding...
Bongos by the bus load
And cungero in tow.

Thumb-bangin-Finger-snappin
Hand-clappin-Foot-tappin

Bad-bass-boogy-Bluesy-mello-funkadello
Rebel-rockrootsy-back-bending-bubble-bass
boogy
With a lil bit of that Shooby-dooby do-wop Wow !
And how !
Smokin and cookin like a Jazz pow-wow.

How the Words were given
Is like how we're Living
From the bubble of Life's Bass
To Love's Basic Rhythm.
Blues moaning and wailing for a love long gone
Strutting sounds standing proud as totemic flag
poles
Peace-pipe fulla that Underground scribble
Scribble on the rhythm keep the poetry living
With some underground scribble.

Call: Good for the Mind!
Response: Good for the Soul!

Call: Good for the Body!
Response: Good for the Soul!

Call: Good for the Spirit!
Response: Good for the Soul!

Call: Good for the People!
Response: Good for the Soul!

And the Beat Goes On! And the Beat Goes On! And
the Beat Goes On! And the Beat Goes On! And the
Beat Goes ......

Jester.

I once saw a Jester...
Wrestling with how best to invest time / Juggling with rhymes / pulling lines and themes of intricately plotted pieces of Kinté cloth / from the misleading emptiness / that hung in the surrounding air.

Multi coloured / Mandinka designs / Adinkra Jazz hues / Now.......
Global and Holistic / Renewed and distinguished by an atmosphere seething with the invisible pregnancy / Of all that is possible.......

And all that is unstoppable.......
I watched as it grew / in varying shapes and sizes / fluttering like the firey wings of manic moths / I watch as effortlessly...

He writes.....
The Diary of / a young Dervish / as a Mad artist / And thats just for starters...he says....

"Seemingly without cause or care/ Out of the nothingness of thin air / Pop mello-toned balloons accompanied by a sun shower of confetti.

Candy striped streamers surge up to a great height / becoming fireworks that explode".

Phallic symbols pop like champagne corks with a bang and a whoosh / Returning to Earth in a cascade of neon lights / Like an advert for patterned tights / And the sights and the sounds of the city at night.

Untill all of a sudden hanging in thin air the Rainbows end from which the seeds of this Carnival shoot forth / An edge that shatters the whole spectrum of preconceived perceptions.

A wonderful yet chaotic light / Piercing the darkness of the nether world...The air / Tinted like the studio mix on the Saturnalian sax solo that pulsates / Where Sun Ra waits in a far off world of abstract dreams like a Lonnie Liston Cosmic Echo or...

A painting by El Greco / Pulsates like a strobe on overload red & yellow & pink & green & purple & orange and blue / Like the cover of the Sam Rivers' album " Hues ".

Incense rises as lilac smoke / Aromatically choking the killing jokers.
Warped perspectives shift into focus.

Paint is splashed around by costumed clowns / Whose faces make you feel like laughing / Even when they frown / A masked Harlequin in a skin-tight suit of diamond patchs / Watchs...

Morocan acrobats in small round hats / rolling under this / jumping over that / trip and stumble / wheel and collapse / As the most delicate set of crystal-ware maidens / Decoratively double as

Egyptian dancing girls / in pink and peppermint / Shining Satin pastel shades...

Their tou-tous amuse / But it is only a ruse to confuse and amaze...
As / They parade the fire and the jade / That only just manages to thinly disguise the newly found menace that glows / through the gentle hues of their flame throwing eyes...

Their garments cling like gracefully flowing garlands scented and sweet to taste / Eyes dance and sinues writhe beneath the lustful lustre of a peach-like pattern of sensual satin / Smooth like the silken hair that flows...

A River of sensuality that sparkles and shimmers salmon leaping and riding the wind / Ending in a pirouette that leaves the atmosphere moist and the very air itself wet / As they fade back into the jumble of the clothes-line jungle

Singing in tune with a samba whistle / Berimbau in hand / There are Bahaian whoops and cheers as Airto Moreira plays a bouncy capoiera / The Jester clears a tear from his eye / smiles and stares...

Laughter fills the air/ A laughter that drowns out the leering-jeers of those who contaminate the / Harvest of The Years / Those who supply the ending that if left unattended would inevitably multiply...

In the bull rushes that stir as hooded eyes

glare / into a miriad of spiralling grapevines/
Each one following its own particular discourse
concerning/ Time/ Loves Rituals/ Each baring
fruits in due season........

Adding Maroon, mauve, magenta, mustard and
ochre. Vermillion, crimson, cream and peuce/
Cobalt, emerald, olive and grey / And all in their
own notorious way / To a never ending heady
season...

Concerning time / loves rituals / and the jugular
vein of Sufitic reason.

Joyful.

Melancholy me?
Not really...
Just quietly happy...
Ask anybody...

At least those who truly know me.

What then do I feel?
Just a sense of joy that I seem to be
Winning this war within me...
And all I know is that now
I feel a lot more real...
Though still reeling from the aftershock
Of that which you randomly unlocked.

And...I thought I could take you on... But you...
You my silently smiling Lady of Mystery

You slayed me…
And it would appear that it's… As plain as daylight
For all to see… Ask anyone… Who can still
recognise me.

Just Dust.

Malamatiyya Mystic Knights
Of Ancient Nishapur
Poets of the people's fight
Poverty at their door...

Humble lions of the Soul
Warriors against their-selves
Blameworthy of hypocrisy
Still they beg to delve...

No rhetoric nor dogma
No rituals nor creed
Just a heart that bleeds
Through an open mind
And the lowliness of weeds...

Vain-glorious ambition
A fire fit for the burning
Their temple is an olive grove
It's fruits were born from yearning.

They say; "Nothing we do ever comes from us
We're just the Salt of the Earth
We're the People of Dust..."

Noone to accuse

Just ourselves to reproach
At the Ka'ba of Heaven
No self-righteous approach...

One heroic journey
One invisible road
No outward appearance
Just a chivalrous code...

Within each heart
Of Life and Love and Learning
Where solitude's no heavy load
And emptiness no burden

All free Souls heed
Their silent call
There is only the One
And it Unites us All...

And they say; "Nothing we do ever comes from us
We're just the Salt of the Earth
We're the People of Dust..."

Kamilz.

On a caravan of camels / the Lovers traveled
Through open spaces / To a cool oasis
Where the belly-dancer boogied / breaking every
rule
To a smooth oudh player / who was blowing his
kool.

Amidst swathes of Shimmering chiffon / a furtive
hint of Khol-mascara
The Seventh veil revealed in shades the
endlessness of the Sahara.
The winds carried / the rhythm of the darrabukka.
Urban Jazz or was it / just North African Jujukka.

Move with the Tide/ Go with the Flow
Enjoy the Ride / The Kamilz Run Slow.

As candle-light twinkled / in the moon-lit medina
Talk turned to tales of olden days / Arabi &
Abysinnia.
Eating cous-cous in the casbah / Savouring the
flavour while it lasted.
Remembrances of humbler days / the reasons why
we've fasted.

The wind beckoned / So we followed
The strangely shifting sands / of our diminishing
tomorrows.
Simple knowledge of the human heart / Dressed in
rags and tatters

We Danced like Dervishes till dawn/ And slept
when we were shattered.

Move with the Tide/ Go with the Flow
Enjoy the Ride / The Kamilz Run Slow.

We were slaves/ then pirates / now we are here
Nomadic spirits but have no fear
With a smile on our lips and an open ear
To our host the message was draw near.
Of all the treasures that we shared that eve
It's rememberance that we hold most-dear.

Move with the Tide/ Go with the Flow
Enjoy the Ride / The Kamilz Run Slow.

Kobuki.

What you did to me
Was spookier than Kobuki
A catastrophe
That I could not have foreseen.

Left with no macho shield
I could do nought but yield
Despite what ever could have
Would have-should have been
You took my heart to the cleaners
And rinsed it clean.

Konobwa.

As my dissolute defenses leave me

Vulnerable
To the whims of my Lady's favour
I feel my Soul grow...

Pregnant with impossibilities
My mind is suffering the pangs
Of an over due labour.

As the damn bursts
I am inundated to the quick
A washed-up Samurai
Spatch-cocked by my own ki'tana
But how? Why?
And in what manner?

Lake Sakinah.

I skim a grey flat pebble across a clear blue lake.
The satin waters ripple
The gentle moonlight wakes
Silence surrounds the gentlest sounds
that shimmer in the stillness.
Soft splashes of expanding rounds
dance with their silent witness.

and I will wait by Lake Sakinah
Listening in the Silence
To the movement of the water
As it ripples in the moonlight...Hmmm...

Sitting still like the pine
On this fragrant night
Serenity deep within my mind

From the depths such a radiant light
Hmmm...
Transparant as the clear blue lake
Shapeless serene and formless
As moonbeams dance in pebbles wake
The silence remains dauntless

and I will wait by Lake Sakinah
Listening in the Silence
To the movement of the water
As it ripples in the moonlight...Hmmm...

Lancashire Hot Spot.

I lick my fingers
When you cook such spices
Pukka lips to suck in air
To calm the steamy kiss
Of a heart that's full of hunger.

For the Ishqish coconut desert
Even the molecules in the air flirt.

Distracted by such passion-Such fire-Such bliss
And all on a moonlit night like this-
All on a moonlit night like this-

Such silence-Such stillness-Such risk...

Lava.

Molten white-Hot...
The earliest bits to break through...

Now solidified into stone cold solid rock...
Painfully hard and decorated
With dangerously sharp edges.

A beach of black volcanic sand
Our place of repose.

We scavenge over the carcass of a dieing
laugh solidified into magma...

Stiff like the hackles on my kneck
when I think .

Activated.

As I waited for your Soul to meet me
Anticipation's rush became psychedelic to the touch
The sea-air felt fresh like the colour green to me, lush
As the silver sound of sea-gulls echoed
In the mauve distance. I was entranced.

The thought of it confused my senses
The sun felt bright across my face
As warm as your pinkness, Miss
As soft as the colour beige in May.
What can I say...

I could hear the swish of your sea shore calling
It's sound as blue as a love swollen police siren
It's taste as kite as the wind
As salt white as tears.

My feet walked like wet woolen socks
As grey as a damp flat Northern cap on a rainy day
My memory of you now a small red-brick chapel
Nestled in a dark dank leafy glade
That smells of protective green shoots
Amidst shifting shadows that felt like
The brown security of the touch of leather.

Recognition Ignition.

There was a recognition ignition
The tide of cause and effect had risen
and it was high time to make a decision
Ism and schism had reared it's dissonant head
And I get less & less time for it the older that I get...

Something inside me said recognise ! Recognise !
Recognise !
And I'm trying to force a reconciliation
Trying to reconcile a situation relating to the
disparate fragments of my inner-most sanctum...
My sanctum-sanctorum if there's enough elders
present then they form a chorum.

The Sanctuary of my Revelrie were in lies a
battered-up old heart with a couple of compound
fractures that contort from time to time as living
testimony to the fact that
Loves not all that's it's sometimes cracked up to be.

And... in my mind
I see that even my original script musta been a bit

ripped
or I musta skipped a bit cos something didn't fit
didn't realise that
that something was me
Cos you see I couldn't see the full picture
Cos I'd been following a fable like it was a scripture.

This is where the Wisdom of the Ancients can come in extremely useful..
Even fruitful......
But first of all of course you have to be truthful with yourself....
For there are some things with which you can not trust anyone else.

As individuals we follow our separate destinies and designated paths waiting to see what each day will proclaim. Days dealt like upturned cards...
Every hand different... No two cards ever the same...

Each card ltself being turned like the pages of a novel
where the anonymous author controls the game play.

Gotta change my expectations to suit whats actually on offer... the Lifestyle of the city places new demands on me to become a new sustainable more viable entity.
Something that agrees with me...At least in theory...

And this is how it is...
Assessing what we may have lost on the way
What we may have accumulated that may have
been of some value
That which was useful or that which we really
needed
from that which we'd thought after and eventually
sought after...
The tears and the laughter...
Your ghetto blaster sings to me
"The Joy The Pain Sunshine & Rain...
Inner-city Life Inner City Pressure".

Inner City pleasure
The sights and the sounds rising up
from the ruins of that which once was once
vibrant...

Still silently burning ...

We turned our gaze skywards on our quest for
Higher learning ...

Compelled by a yearning ... or something beyond
the realms of the senses...

Something that heals us and helps us Grow.

And never mistake the life of the heart as mere Art
for it is a Living Thing... Like the tiny silver & black
jet-stone ring
that you wear on the wrong finger...

If you kill the Heart ... it's body may depart...
But believe me it's ghost will linger.
And this is how it is... with us...

Love's Witness Testifies.

It's not where you think your coming from
It's not even where your at
It's what's written deep within your own heart
If you can just get to that
It's not the many masks that we like wearing
It's not anything that you can name
Cos it lives beyond all of our Earthly rituals
And the rules change with the game
Hmmm ! Hmmm ! Hmmm ! Hmmm !

And I wouldn't like to tell you how this things identified
Cos I know from past experience that it can't be quantified
Loves is endlessly unfolding and it can't be analysed
Love is vast and love's eternal
And it can not be denied !
Hmmm ! Hmmm ! Hmmm ! Hmmm !

It's not just about a feeling
Or a sad and happy glow
You can't capture it with meaning
Cos that's not the way it flows
It's not even linked to resaon

Mind's get trapped within their creeds
And it's not the phony piety
That smiles while poor folks bleed.
Hmmm ! Hmmm ! Hmmm ! Hmmm !

And I wouldn't like to tell you how this things
identified
Cos I know from past experience that it can't be
quantified
Loves is endlessly unfolding and it can't be
analysed
Love is vast and love's eternal
And it can not be denied !

Maritime Pine.

An unknown marine-scape has slowly taken
shape.
Coral pink fronds flirt with the retreating
shoreline.
Maritime pines Mambo along a curious coast,
A beach full of scallop shells, edges tinged
tangerine,
Presents a scene as mysterious as the changing
climate.
And in my empathy I practice a continuity of
reinvented memories
Of how things used to be…
Each building once as substantial as a mango tree .

Radiant as ever the sun breaks through the
dancing tree-tops

Firing golden shafts of light deep into the heart of this wooded lagoon
Scattering shadows across the rippling shallows
That swirl around the moss covered rock pools.

At the edge of the forest
I hear you listening to the seas Eternal rhythm
As it swishes in the hearts of mermaids, mice and men...
Slender ferns draw dark stripes across an oatmeal strip of land.
The dunes a quilt of russets, mossy-greens, and orangey tans,
Mixed with sand.

Deep within there is a stillness / a knowing / a presence.
Golden adventure rising in the blood
Song running like a river through the heart's silver veins
The enveloping water ringing with The Pristine Names.

There is a freshness in the air. A sense of beginning.
All around me ... The water rises... the horizon beckons.
At the centre of the forest / I sense you / move closer.
Somewhere within the serenity
Of nature's secrets slowly revealed ... As sure as the waters cover the Earth...

Love heals.

Masaala.

Time stopped by the Green man Khidr-
A tyrant and a tamed unicorn covered in green moss-
Both lost in their discoveries
Inventing the wheel anew
High above the ignominy of this suburban slavery...
I wait for you.
You wait for me...
A rhapsody of blue embroidery
An angel with a raven's look
A raven with an angel's hook
Angelic moonlight.
Eastern cook
Masaala by gaslight.
Loves own book.

Modern Life.

Culturally modern life is !
Is... a multi-dimensional / Pan-Racial / Cross-cultural / Hybrid experience / Of uncharted head spaces and unclassifiable creeds / Non-denominational / Inter-subjective / Interfacing / yet / Stylstically functioning / Divergent streams / of crosspollinatory fractals / where occasionally something gells / Full on Human divergence and

real Human meaning that transcends the bullshit.

Oral Poesie.

The rhythms and melodies of our speech.
Our mother Tongue, our metalanguage, our Love.
Ancestral Wisdom from an Oral Tradition
That's open to anyone
Real enough to listen
With a Heartical vision.

Everything Fades.

Everything fades but the face of Allah.
Everything fades but the face of my Lord.
Everything fades but the face of Allahu!
Al Hay-Ul Qayyum!

Lailaha-ila-Allahu!
Allah ! His names and His traces.
The Majesty and Awe
The Compassion and Grace.
That which... elevates The Soul.
Al Jamal wa'l Jalal.
That which let's us know that there is more to Life
Than our feet of clay...
More to the Spirit than it's possible to say...
More to Humanity than we can ever achieve...
More to the weft and more to the weave...

Of each Diverse existence that's ever been
concieved...

For example... as an instance...
Sakinah! Wijdan Karama!
Silence! Discovery! Miracles!

Each unknowable possibility
Of Life's ultimate reality...
Is but a mere manifestation
Of the endless variegations
Of the Breath of the Compassionate...

That animates and permeates...
The Whole World within that which it emanates.

Everything fades but the face of Allah.
Everything fades but the face of my Lord.
Everything fades but the face of Allahu!
Al Hay-Ul Qayyum!

Every village - Every home town - Every country -
Every nation, race, tribe, and city state of the art...
Every variation of Human potential.
None of it is coincidental.

Every permutation of Life's limitless equations
Continually flowing & unfolding
Like the Ikhtiar of a Jazz Aria
Each Soul a spark from the original fire.
The Tashkeel of the Living and the Real.

Every permeation of conscious awareness
That we see - hear - taste - detect the scent of or feel
They all come from Allah's Rahmah.
The Love that is... Ar Raheem
The Womb of The Real.

No caste! No class! No colour! No creed! No need!
Dogma deadens the mind.
Seek beyond the borderlines
Seek and you will find
A parallel place in a timeless time.

No flag, no badge, no banner, no label, no tag.
No exclusive club of uncharted headspaces.
No faces that don't fit...
Only Divine traces from the Sacred places.

I'm contemplating my non-existence.
Realising why I'm really nothing at all.
I'd like to make that point quite clear.
I'm an empty picture on an empty wall.

Everything fades but the face of Allah.
Everything fades but the face of my Lord.
Everything fades but the face of Allahu!
Al Hay-Ul Qayyum!

Moments.
(A vocalese version of Chet Baker's Stolen Moments).

As I wander I look over my shoulder,
To see where I've been comin' from
It's a habit I learned by growing older,
Keep my back to the settin' sun.

All the fears that we hide
Buried deep with the tide
All the times that we've lied
All the tears we've denied

About feelings inside
For the sake of our pride...
Lost to the hands of time!
Precious Moments-Precious Moments.

Some tales go on & on they're condescending.
It would seem that's how seasons flow.
Time is always so very never ending.
As if Time alone truly knows

But your eyes shine with kindness
That eases my blindness
And helps me to find this !
And hold this ! And time this !
Align this ! Design this !
And polish and shine this...
'Til it feels like mine!
Precious Moments-Precious Moments.

In my silence I'm searching for the moments
Where the truths that are left untold
Linger always just waiting to be opened
Some start fires ! Some leave you cold !
All the tatters of patterns
We've scattered don't matter
They flatter the fashion
"Of just how it happens"
Cos now that your nearer
It's clearer to see...
The moving hand of Time!
Precious Moments-Precious Moments.

Morning Song.

When the birds sing at dawn
There is no irritation
No derision nor scorn
Just their Soul's fascination...
Hmmm... Hmmm... Hmmm ...

It's the language of love
That's beyond imitation
There not really forlorn
It's just pure adoration...
Hmmm... Hmmm... Hmmm ...

Nothing but validation
There is nothing but you
Not even negation....

Mother of Pearl.

Love's Solitary Pearl is the purpose of Life's test
The folly of youth's Quest.... is a grain of Cosmic
sand
stuck in the crabmeat craw of an afro-dizziak
chorister.

Sometimes eaten raw... like an oyster.
The passive catalyst that potently produces the
Grist...
for the natural metamorphosis of nightclub into
cloister.

Love's purity of purpose that carries us higher
Than the octopus of our all too human desires.
The Soltary Pearl is a crescent shaped sphere of
grace and compassion...
A singular symbol of contemplation / the
completeness / the satisfaction.

As sure as the trees in the woodland whistle / and
sparkle like starlight for all to see
Like me loving you and you loving me.
In an unjust an transient World / the shell of our
Faithfulness unfurled
Existentially revealing...
Just a Solitary Pearl.

"One Love".

A story to be sung our personal culture.
The individual in the cacophonous city.
Invisible as a grain of sand on a Beach.
An anonymous anomaly, amidst...
The mutated mélanges of the metropolis.
Soul secreted deep within the golden silences.
Of these silent city streets.
Sakinah, as still as a human heart beat.

To be Centered, but drifting like a cloud
No mind , no tears, no thoughts, no blame.
Not even a haunting refrain. Just... a
A solitary pearl. A rose perchance...A Soul...
Exuding the serene elixir of life's

Purest of poetics.
A diamond spark of light...
From somewhere hidden...
Within ...the stillness, the silence, the emptiness

A one amongst millions non-entity enraptured
By the womb of the formless.
The serenity of the Eternal moment...
That is always now. Hu Wu Mu.
Suspended in time, but forever flowing like water.
The synchronistic and the serendipitous.
Wu-Wei. The non-being of bliss.

I'm happy being nobody son of no-one.
Gone with the wind and dispersed in the rain.
I'll live and I'll die but my Spirit will flow on...
As sure as love is both sacred, and profane.

Sibilance.

In the beginning was the word
And it was delivered with sibilance to aid
remembrance
Knowledge knowingly wrapped in music so we
wouldn't loose it.

The Tassawufman from Tareem said
"Speak soft words and show forth your excellence."

And our music is our culture
Is who we are... Is our Spirit...
Our past present and future, carried here from
afar.

And our proof is in the proud sound
Of pounding hearts
As they relate the evidence of our all too Human
history.

An all too murky mystery.
That neither begins nor ends with the Mersey or
you or me.

Resistance being reconfigured daily with the
utmost glee
In sympathetic symphonies that are as related to
The Celestial rhapsodies of the spheres.
As: The Word is to the tongue
As: Right is to Wrong
As: The pen is to the ink
As: Harmony is to a Gracious gift that helps us to
see
And guides how we think.

Angelic emissions of sound-vision engender
Melodic light-forms of Universal rhythm.
And...
Our Music Is... Our Struggle Is ... Our Survival Is...
Our Mother Tongue... Is... Our Path... Is Our Belief

Jazz-zhikr and scholarship fused
As the crooning camel herder broods
Bilal's Ethiopian Call to Prayer
And Negro spirituals fill the air
Habashi-Gospel related Blues
Clues to our Abysinian dues.

Nat Turner's heritage
Firmly rooted in Oral Revelation
The legacy of a hard working chain of transmission
Voices that testified to the Truth of our Human condition.
Related to what ?
Related to the Malcolm Devotee whose Jazz poetry
Taught some of my Homies and Me to say the Takbir !
And magnify our Lord Most High, loud and clear.

Angelic emissions of sound-vision engender
Melodic light-forms of Universal rhythm.
And...
Our Music Is... Our Struggle Is ... Our Survival Is...
Our Mother Tongue... Is... Our Path... Is Our Belief

Suleiman's Wisdom our dependance in toil and struggle.
Abraham's Religion our endurance in turmoil and strife
Haji Malik as-Shabazz brought us back to The Sunnah
With the rhythms and tones of our everyday life.

Coltrane's lived experience as retold thru his saxophone
Helped Malcolm hone the rhythms and polyphonies of African speech tones
Cos he knew what it needed to drive the message home.

Through our music we'll never walk alone.

Angelic emissions of sound-vision engender
Melodic light-forms of Universal rhythm.
And...
Our Music Is... Our Struggle Is ... Our Survival Is...
Our Mother Tongue... Is... Our Path... Is Our Belief

Music in the Soul regulates the hearts beat
To the rhythm of The Universe where all Soul's meet.
Silence-Sound Opposites abound
Rhythm functions inbetween - Recreates the middle ground
This is where most Wisdom's found.

Melody and rhythm binding chapter and verse
The language of the Spirit that is unrehearsed
And who God bless let no man curse.
And don't nobody praise me till you done seen my worst.

Angelic emissions of sound-vision engender
Melodic light-forms of Universal rhythm.
And...
Our Music Is... Our Struggle Is ... Our Survival Is...
Our Mother Tongue... Is... Our Path... Is Our Belief
Is who we are.

Biti Benafi / Good Morning.
(Written for Cardiff Mas Carnival show "Exodus." Biti Benafi is Garifuna.)

Chorus: On paradise island
the sun says "Good Morning"
"Biti Benafi"
a new day is dawning.

solo voice: Humming birds hover
by sweet mango trees
whose fragrance rides
the cool ocean breeze.
Water falls freely
from clear mountain streams.
Flying fish spiced
and cooked to a dream.

chorus: On paradise island
the sun says "Good Morning"
"Biti Benafi"
a new day is dawning.

solo voice: Old folks relaxing
children at play
Nothing is taxing
at this time of day.
growing cassava
and working the sea
A life close to nature
a life-style so free.

chorus: On paradise island
the sun says "Good Morning"
"Biti Benafi"
a new day is dawning.

Path.

A snaking black wet tarmac path
Precedes my tracks as I walk fast
Through seas of green above the dell
Where thickets hide the wishing well.
There secrets rest where lost coins dwell
Warm tongues relate what fortunes tell.

The clouds grow grey the sky breaks forth
A cold wind blows from Winter's North.
Hope springs anew from deep within
Stark solstice ends fresh growth begins.

Bathe in lifes stream renew the light
Love's dreams reborn sung in the night.
All time is gain we can but win
Premeditate the good within.

The Crystal Flow.

Where the crystal waters flow
Greener shoots usher forth.
Pure light springs from between the rocks
And clean air cools the thoughts.

A fountain of brilliance as sweet to the soul
Dew-drops shimmering fresh with spring
And love is a sigh that floats on the wind
As gentle as the sound of a butterfly's wing.

Refreshing as a mountain lake or an alpine stream

That water's the soul with what Sweet-Hearts know.
A fragrant fountain of sparkling dreams.

Reflections of the sacred flow.
We are always our own worst enemy
  Too easily influenced like everyone else
By the times and the trash on the telly
That keeps us from our inner-self.
Verdiant pastures of the graceful unseen
The Natural The Tranquil The Subtle The Serene

Shadows's scatter like moths before the radiant might of
The Most High, The Vast, The Eternal, The Light.

The Pearl.

It's summertime and the Pearl has become
a perfect sphere
that glows
with an irredescant white light.
Yet remains…
as colourless as sound
as shapeless as Human sight.

Focussed light
passing thru the crystal pyramid.
Prismatic enhancement.
Clarity of vision an invisible force.
A spectrum of perceptions in tangible precision.

Where these seven seas become The Endless Sea

There's an Ocean of possibility...
And all barriers have ceased to be.
Somewhere in this vicinity Love flows...
Without resistance
As effortlessly as a dolphin swims
Towards the coll clear air of
It's natural existance.

From the depths to the shallows
That invite the dancing Sun to play...
Tip and run across silver crests.
Golden light ignites life. fire meets ice.
Where dancing sunbeam's stop to rest.

And there is Tauhid in the nature inherent in the silence...
Of a solitary pearl / a reflection of the radiance.
Out of which this Oneness of Love and Life
Has arisen.

Placed in the sun-light caringly.
The Oneness alone will glisten.

Away from the heedlessness that leads to The Hour.
You will hear it if you listen.

On That Day.

Oh I swear by the afterglow of sunset
By the night when it enshroudeth
By the clouds when they forget

Oh when the sun is overthrown and the stars fall
And the mountains turn to rubble and Mother
earth calls.
When the seas rise upon the land and the jungles
turn to sand
When the trees stand up and have their say
And when the skies and the heavens are torn away.

On that day on that day there'll be nothing left to
say.
On that day on that day there'll be nothing left to
sayiayay.

When the Earth reveals up her stories and the
graves give up their dead
When we hear our Souls repent for all the vain
things we have said
When Earth's creatures group together and the
moon turns red
And the planets are called to witness and every
tears been shed.

On that day on that day there'll be nothing left to
say.
On that day on that day there'll be nothing left to
sayiayay.

When the heavens are torn asunder and the
planets are dispersed
And the oceans are poured forth and the
sepulchers are overthrown
A Soul will know what it has sent before it and
what it has left behind

Lo Allah's angels are generous in recording the
Endless Time.

On that day on that day there'll be nothing left to
say.
On that day on that day there'll be nothing left to
sayiayay.

Pirate Cove.

So many things since then
Have spoken volumes to me

Made my heart feel light
Set my pirate's brig free

From the dark dank harbour
Where I'd long ago dropped anchor.

Wind in my sail's once again
I bathe daily in the warm ocean
Of Love's serendipity.

Sailing on synchronicity
I ride life's silver crests with zest
Yet ever so nonchalantly.

Wild Frontier Blues.

You accuse me of possession
Of a shady disposition
You avoid my eyes
And your nose is a' twitchin'
Your ears seem closed

To the things that I'm sayin'
But right now my favourite
Radio stations playin'
Hmmm...

It's a Cowboy World / And it aint no news
This is the Wild Frontier / Wild Frontier Blues
Yippy Kaiyo-kaiyayay-ay ! / Yippy Kaiyo-kaiyayay-
ay !
Yippy Kaiyo-kaiyayay-ay ! / But what does Tonto
have to say...

It's a Cowboy World / And it aint no news
This is the Wild Frontier / Wild Frontier Blues
Yippy Kaiyo-kaiyayay-ay ! / Yippy Kaiyo-kaiyayay-
ay !
Yippy Kaiyo-kaiyayay-ay ! / But what does Tonto
have to say...

You say I've got an attitude
That causes friction
All I'm hearing from you
I call it science fiction
Forever's a long time
We got distance to cover
We can't stop now
We might never recover...
Hmmm...

You say I'm a mad dog
Runnin' with the rabble
I'm the Mohawk in the woodpile
I was born as rebel

Aint no sign-posts on the road
That we'all travel
I kinda likes it that way
It kinda keeps us level...
Hmmm...

It's a Cowboy World / And it aint no news
This is the Wild Frontier / Wild Frontier Blues
Yippy Kaiyo-kaiyayay-ay ! / Yippy Kaiyo-kaiyayay-ay !
Yippy Kaiyo-kaiyayay-ay ! / But what does Tonto have to say...
Heyah-Heyah ! Heyah-Heyah ! Heyah-Heyah !

Poetry Blues.

I started writing poetry / A long-long time ago.
I used to write in pencil / Now I use a biro.
I published a slim volume / With money from the arts
Match funded by the council / That's how I got my start.

I let the people be my witness !
Cos you can't trust big business !
No Way!

I once studied polemics / Read comics and told jokes.
Spoke to an audience of One / Wrote for the common folks.
Quotes to fill a bin liner / Rhymes to fill a bin bag.

One or two good one liners / With the antlers of a stag.

I let the people be my witness !
Cos you can't trust big business ! No Way!

Puma.

At night the Light is all there is.
It is here that I meet
She who hunts without weapons.
It is here that she waits for me.
Perfumed predator
In the uncharted depths of darkness
Illuminated by the silver light of the Feminine Moon

A beige puma
eyes of smoking jade
leaves a semi circle
of neat red-currant dints
in a soft toffee shoulder.

These in time turning
to tiny purple glyphs.
Each containing
the concentrated meaning
of a thousand sacred scrolls.
Sweet scented water
from an ancient well

Poirot.

Coffee and cardamom / Very Arabian
Spit in the sand / Well I'll be damned
Dates and lamb ? I don't understand
Is that the way the Beloved planned.

To know God in person
Helps to keep the heart working.

Pupation.

We distilled the nectar
of the
Eternal Presence.

spinning ribbons
around each other
in a
silken swathe
of
mutual osmosis.

The vitalities of our Life force
blending perfectly.

Grace pupating into...
a chrysalis
Our cocoon composed
of the sugar coated crystals

Given Time / the Nature of Things / & the
Changing Seasons
The rose bud of our relationship
flowered into a butterfly...

Compelling & beautiful to behold
still ever elusive.

Serenity.

Silence is the gateway to Serenity
Letting go of the moment to just simply "Be !"
Like a leaf on the wind or the wind in the trees
The keeper of Life's Sacred mysteries.

Focused in prayer may this Joy never cease
Lighter than air may the blessings increase
Sweet Soul in submission may your Heart be
released
Into the tranquil Sovereignty of Inner Peace.

Service with Love is its own reward
For there is Joy in the smile from which Hearts are
secured... For to serve one another is to serve your
Lord
Wherein all fear is waylaid and all Hope restored.

I am Silence, I am Sovereignty, I am Service.
I am a Soul at Peace working out my purpose.
So let my name be... Let my name be... Let it be...
Serenity, Serenity, Serenity !
Silence Defined as Light.

Silence.

Silence is a place
where one finds

the inner space
to unwind
deep within the confines
of the the tired mind
the inner eye of humankind
shines

sometimes shimmering
so brightly
that it blinds;

Space to reflect
on life's side effects...
an island where we construct
rafts from the hopes and dreams
that are
or have been
marooned and shipwrecked.

A place
where we merely sit and listen...
And measure each grain of sand
that the incessant sea casts upon
the beach of our beatitude
at leisure...
slowly
softly
silently...
in silence.

A place where...
if... we have faith
we discover

hidden treasure

And drink a toast
to that which matters most
playing host to the tranquility
and the solitude
that nurtures peace...
as knowing replaces speech
and silence grants us release.

Soul Shine.

The Swallows that the Summer brought us
Echo Cuckoo's mellowed rhymes
Starlings sip from crystal waters
Thrush sings parsley, sage and time...

The Magpies jamming and the joy they bring
Wood Pidgeons wooing words relax
But this Raven flies on broken wings
It's feet of clay remain attached...

Lone Nightingales enshrine in sound
Finches furtive liason
Crow's flattery runs truth to ground
The Seagulls cry "Oh ! Vain one !"...

The Hawk cries "Death is where it starts!"
Rook's acrid squawk ensures us
Love's Dove descends into our hearts
Sweet Sparrows sing songs for us

Sunny Sunday's Soulful Shine

Birdsong Blending in with mine
And I'mso glad to be alive
At this Sunny Sunday Soul Shine.

Spark.

I've found it again
that golden light.

I've felt it again
that shere delight.

I've sensed it again
the heart took flight.

A tangerine sun tints
A blue misty night.

Storm.

There's a storm out tonight / and I kinda like it
Have'nt seen you in ages, Baby / and I'm not gonna
fight it
I respect the tempest / it's in tune with my mood
The moon is rising tempestuous / as wild as the
wood.

Blow North Wind blow !
Blow North Wind Blowowowo !
Blow North Wind blow !
Blow North Wind Blowowowo !

Wish you were here / where the wild wind howls
Be my Lady Guinevere / on this night fit for growls

Roof tiles crash to the ground / people rush to their windows
This weather's sure to confound , Baby / it's as if the wind knows.

Blow North Wind blow !
Blow North Wind Blowowowo !
Blow North Wind blow !
Blow North Wind Blowowowo !

There's something in the air / seems like the wind of change
The atmosphere is clear / my aims got more range
We could take to the wing / on an evening like this
We could dance and sing, Baby / where the tree roots twist.

Blow North Wind blow !
Blow North Wind Blowowowo !
Blow North Wind blow !
Blow North Wind Blowowowo !

Sugar and Spice.

It took a long time to work out
Cos it's hard to understand
That it's as simple as you like
It's just never like you planned.

Let's try to see where we went wrong
So we can put things right
Self-reflection makes us strong
What weakens us is lies.

We're here and it could be beautiful
We're here and it could be oh so nice.
Let's try to make the most of it
Now hand me some of that
Sugar and Spice.

Vain discourse drains the brain
Circumstantial & conclusive
But with the right surroundings
The environments condusive
To what is most important
What relates to who we are
What's tied up with our Destiny
What is written in our Hearts.

Sunlight.

Pine needles underfoot
The scent of sand
Clouds as pure as milk

A headiness like spring subdued me
As it soothed my senses smooth as silk

Pleasing to the eye like the colour of dawn
The mid-morning sun
breaks through the thickets
Scattering sunbeams
like wild fire

An angelic light piercing the forest's darkest veils
You can not commodify this experience

This is not for sale

And at such times much healing takes place
So it is with us

Our Mother Earth.

Corporate red tape covers climate debate

Some people are saying it's already too late.

Endangered species all over the place

Top of the list is theyre saying is the Human Race.

We have to prove our worth / And heal our Mother
Earth

We have to prove our worth / And heal our Mother
Earth

Our Mother Earth... Our Mother Earth!

Oh woe woe I ! Oh woe I

Plastic in the desert plastic in the seas

Plastic in the islands and the Arctic freeze

Plastic in the oceans, rivers, and seas

Polluting Creation like a deadly Disease.

The Rain Forest home off Indigenous tribes

Laid waste by greed, propaganda and lies.

Corporate criminals with their eyes on the prize

And no one is saying just how many have died.

We have to prove our worth / And heal our Mother Earth

We have to prove our worth / And heal our Mother Earth

Our Mother Earth... Our Mother Earth!

Oh woe woe I ! Oh woe I !

Freedom sounds coming down along the way / No matter what they do and no matter what they say.

Freedom sounds coming down along the way / No matter what they do and no matter what they say.

From Shades of Slack to Starker Tones.

I could have called this collection of contemporary urban Slack orature/ The Muted Palette/ or A Deeper Shade of Stark as opposed to a Triter shade of pale/ or is that a Politer Shade of Pale in which case it would have been a Slacker shade of Stark/ on a more subtle note I thought maybe Jazz conversations/ or Jazz conversations in the Key of X/ Blue Notes in the Key of Life/ or X even / Slack Notes in the Key of X/ Slack Voices/ Slack Sketches/ Charcoal/ Perfume for the Slack Soul/ Jazz Notes / Blue Notes/ Scribble/ Scribble on the Rhythym/ Underground Scribble/ Jazz Scribble/ Hardfunkin/ Slamdunkin dribble/ hard-core not liberal/ well maybe a little bit liberal with a small ' L '/ Urban Jazz Creatures/ Urban Jazz Preaching/ Slack Ink/ Ink Screeching/ Pen Preaching/...

What I needed...

you see was a title that is/ was something to clue you in/ something to give you an insight into where I'm coming from...where the poetry is coming from/ or this collection anyway (and if your already there you'll have noticed a host of intertextual In House/ references and at least two references to Stevie Wonder material for those who know his work/ not to mention some of your more avante garde Jazz poets/ experimental musicians/ artists etc/ Art Ensemble of Chicago/ Sun Ra/ Gill Scott Heron/ The Last Poets/ Amiri Baraka-Leeroy Jones/ Ishmael Reed/ Kalamu Ya Salam/Don L. Lee/ Haki Madabuthi/Bruce Lee/ Jackie Chan...

Yeah ! that's right Bruce Lee and Jackie Chan/ As I was saying before I started to preempt my critics, I throw more stuff like that in as I go along...

I may thow in stuff lie the Phol Rennaisiance Ensemble, or the York Waits, or The Agincourt Hymn, or Shakespeare, or Marlow, Walt Whitman, Joyce, Pound, Elliot, Picasso, Monet, El Greco, Tallis, Hildegarde de Bingh, Simone De Bouvoir, Gertrude Stein, I'd list them all if I had the time/ I mean there's an endless line of people waiting to be quoted including people like Jung, Fromm, and especially Eistein...

And I throw them in just as an example of what may be for some people, some of the more accessible/salient cultural references/ points where Slack culture crossed over to "popular" i.e. the commercial world, and as such became available to/ well basically to Polite-folks as well/ just to give some of you an inroad to the general ancestry of this type of stuff...

If you aint there already I need to position you the

reader to know what to expect/ The point being suspend your expectations/ What it is ! Is What it is! And its like that cos that's the way it is/ Those who know'll know / And / I mean...

If you don't know about contemporary Urban Slack vibes/ or Slack culture/ Slack style then you may miss some of this put across/ communication.

This exercise in strategic non-essentialism... Essentialy exercising a bit of spontaneous complexity. What the Sufis call Ikhtiyah / spontaneous utterances / abstract inspirations from No-Mind / the All Mind. It's all mined from the Gold mine. Do you really mind?

No idea what most people will make out of it/ but even then can anyone really guarantee understanding/ or take the intended communicative potential of a particular text for granted/ especially something that's aimed at a pan-cultural audience.

The facts are that sadly not everybody will be able to catch my drift/ that's why I often find myself contextualizing and explaining all the time/ its something that as a Slack person, you are forever having to do. Why? Because if you don't Polite-folks just don't understand/ sometimes if you do they don't understand.

This is a Slack thing/ Slack-folks have no choice

other than to be brought up being reminded everyday where Polite-folk's society is coming from/ Some complacent poetry enthusiast me of having a chip/ I had to remind him/It was Polite-folks that brought us here in the first place/ as such ' We ' is always being judged in relation to where ' They ' is at/ They been running our show ever since the days of slavery one way or another/ So now/ we search for ways to define our selves/style/ say in our own way.

We are often asked for definitions/ definitions that we do not need/ not to create/ to create Ha !/ We operate in a different way/ respond to different impulses/ all Slack people have a story to tell/ a story that links us all/ and we like to read something that speaks to our experience/ something that speaks to our experience because it comes from our experience/ The Slacker it is the more we like it because what we like is to see ourselves/ Our Slack selves/ as we are/ Free from captivity/ Free from the hegemonistic, albeit well meaning liberal minds who would like to redesign us in accordance to what they can handle/ A something that will always judge us in relation to them being the norm/ God Love them/ Seriously / These people are looseing their grip and arresting their own development / Long term evolutionary / Morphic Resonance / Deep History ...

The balls in motion already/ We decide what reality is for ourselves/ Those same selves that were beaten into submission on the plantations/ denied education in the cities/ subjected to colonialisation in their own homes/ and given no choice except to fight for emancipation/ and even today the struggle aint over and the fighting aint through.

So we just do what we do/ and we all understand that this is what we gotta do/ We do what we do, cos we do and that's the way is/ the way its always been/ for us/ And if you don't like it then hey... Good Luck to you feh tru. The noo.

If you need a definition/ You can define this style as............. (write suggestion on the dotted line).

The attitude as Hip-Hop/ Rap is another way/ a close relative in fact a descendant of Jazz poetry and prose and of course Gospel and the Blues all the way back to the Negro Spirituals that my Momma loved so much... along with Poppa's home grown Country R & B stuff/ CHECK Out my MA dissertation for an in depth explanation of the form and its ancestry...

In the Senegambia region of Ancient Mali/ Failing that just suspend all Eurocentric notions of form/ The Content is the Form/ this is a Slack norm...there is an essay by a Jazz poet/ Eugene Samuel Lange-Golden, Flo Lange's lad, L'il Gene .aka Muhammadu Khalilu... yeah that's me feh tru / An Essay entitled... " What makes Slack Poetry in the U.K. Slack and U.K. "

Somewhere in there is a preface to this linguistic JAM SESSION/ And it all adds up to the roots of this genre stemming from the Slack oral tradition/ Yes this is a Jam session/ a free flowing no way of knowing unless you follow the way the river is going rapidly applied poetic showing and telling of why it really don't matter how I say or the way I'm spelling my way around the problems faced by speaking a Slack experience with Polite sounds/ Not to mention trying to write it all down about What it is being what it is cos its like that cos That's the Way It Is/ Dig ?

But anyway let me just say this/ For the sake a new tomorrow and a brighter day that sees the end of some of the negative things I've said or may even be about to say stick around and don't be no clown and dig what your anonymous, omniscient narrator is throwing down as I unravel my flex and kick into this watery text by introducing myself...

Hi ! I'm your Griot, Djelá, Jelefo, Jare, Jali, Gavel/Halamkat, storyteller, Boss Talker, cultural-historian, Bluesman, B-boy , your D.J. / Interlocuter, Toaster, Boaster, Bull Shitter and Roaster, Heartical Chanter that'll take you on a roller coaster with some Spiritual bnter.

Your Soul M.C./ that's me...

Narrator X, Jazzbo, loud mouth Negro, Bongo Red, Wolfshead / Dhe Dub Maestah, Blues Dervish, Sufi

Soul singing Jazzgriot in a freestyle word flow/
And...

As I was saying/ about the title/ I think I'll call it
From Shades of Slack to Starker Tones.

Yeah ! I like that/ its arty but it gets a little closer to
the facts/ Cuts a little closer to the bone.
From Shades of Slack to Starker Tones. Yeah !

Yeah I might even keep all of this hit and call it a
poem.
A free-style poem entitled;

From Shades of Black to Darker Tones. Yeah !

The Place.

Dhe Place dhat exists
dhat iz not like any utha place
or
anythin' else...
I know dhat place...
I carry id around widh me...
I wear id sometimes as a musk oil...
I listen to id in me hedset...
Some of me favorite
sounds
when produced from a tenor saxophone
speak to me
of id...
Id has a pattern
like dhe tiles in dhe Al Rahmah mosque

in
Toxteth...
a shape like a secret smile...
Id hops like a tree frog
to
dhe echo-plex ricochet of a militant rim-shot
playin' hard-core steppers
like a red chillie pepper
id
Hot! Hot! Hot!
A colour whose existance in dhe British Isles
can no longer be denied...
a taste like black-peppered chicken well-fried...
kinda cultural and nice like red beans & rice
& a smell like sensi dhats hard to hide...
A texture like kinté clothe
with a raised pattern
A feelin'...
dhat dhere's more to life dhan
What dhey say is happenin'
I know dhat place
It's called in my own skin.

East Berlin.

post apocalyptic aesthetics
resurrected amidst
bullet strafed bricks...

an avant garde-heaven
in the heavily run down
retro-here and now...

a place where the past
catches up
with it self
in ways that havn't been
thought of in some places...

grey is sort of in...abundance...

Mad Max Caf·

a junky staggers into
a low-budget sculpture park...
fronted by the Mad-Max caf·
big solid recycled log tables

welded metal chairs
everywhere welded metal
everywhere an allusion
to weight of some sort
hangs in the air.

Eastern Europe is here...
where we stop for a bowl

milch coffee
a beef and pickle bagette

in a caf· that forms
part of a kunst halle
funded by the British Council...
we chill...and hold council...service is slow.........

next morning at breakfast
at a little Italian pavement
caf·/ we will discuss how all
the staff are voluntary
that   explains   why   the   service   is   so
slow...

great furniture though
a nice place to do a gig
maybe   next
time......Maybe...

Mad-to the Max seed/ psychosis serialised/ and
spat out onto the street as graffiti...product of
the Riechstaag/ the Nurembereg Rallies/ and at a
guess the Warsaw treaty...

a psyche in distress dressed up as art and/ spat out
onto the street as graffiti...for poets and Africans
to relate to and connect with/ a discussion
in Hambourg/ about spirituality/ Islam/ Sufism/
and spirit dust...she said.......spirit dust must be a
German thing we thought...

combination tea/ peppermint and something/
whose taste we did not notice/ name we did

not recognise and a freelance journalist/ half German half Ivory Coast/ a hostess with the most intellectual approach/ from a range of serious sisters/ blakculture witnesses...relatives on a level relate..

and I'm back in Berlin/ I try but the reality defies my category due to a specifically Berlin flavoured homogeneity/ the sounds of post industrial angst/ match the ranks that file out in misadventure playground.../ everything is post......................................

the only thing happening at present/ not the present in that specifically Berlin flavoured space/ but the broader present that represents the Delicious Do-nuts sense of taste/ seems to be...........

the sounds of somewhere else/ Jamaica/ Africa/ Rio de Janiero and Bahai/ Liverpool 8/ but that won't be untill later.......then my lyrics really kick in...Soul on Ice/ becomes trans-cultural...although I am unaware of it at this point in time..

tomorrow will take me forward...it will be a watershed of sorts/ and I will become my own imaginary fortune teller/ the one I was as a school boy/ stylistically unresolved/ but evolving beyond that which I have learned to do so well that it bores me/ sometimes to the point of dispair...nutter yes thats right but I don't care......................

(3)

I learn about Eastlers and Westlers/ tollerance/ Thorsen and Alia/ Anya and a disabled girl called Simone tells me of a Polish Rasta commune in Poland/ Naturally...they make Nyah Bhingi drums/ she drums Nyah/ a Naphtali wearing the colours of a Levite/ She has never heard of the Twelve Tribes/ purple and green mean nothing to her/ she plays burrah but prefers repeater/ Ras Michael and the Twinkle Bros where there/ an eight kilometer walk from anywhere/ we wan goh deh...we affee goh deh...
Insha'Allah..

(4)

The beef and pickle bagette tastes good/ I was hungry/ the sounds of post industrial angst/ and out in misadventure playground...the warning in German says it all/ you enter this private-public space at your own risk/ a bombed out bohemia/ the type of place...where all is not well...
and a sign post that tells you your half-way/ to hell/ cos...well...all is not well..

a hypodermic nightmare built from days gone by........................
Herman Brood/Lou Reed... Bowie... The Bauerhaus and the dance of a decades relentless decadance.../ leaves an after taste that has become characteristic

of this place but like the poem says even/ here blak culture brings the sunshine with it/ sows the seeds of resistance/ gives the alternative colours with which to paint a bouquet of possiblities...endless realities/ that challenge the greyness and the grey reminiscent of uniforms of another long gone day...................

Thorns.

Epeé displayed
I stand centre stage
Only to be upstaged
By your ecstatic rage.

"Purple Silk enfolds the Gold and the Jade
That rests in Oak tree's green satin shade...
A passionate peuce the jungle-juice
That seeps from hearts impaled on Life's blade."

Venus as a veritable Valkyrie
Ever so demurely Taking afternoon tea.
Savoring the almond scented after taste
Intimacy lurking Ninja-like
Somewhere between Love and Hate.

Love caught in the centre of
A Vortex that vacillates with the voluptuous
Eruptions of Vesuvius's Volcanic Vulva
We played Mastermind the Deluxe version
And various shades of Charades
Untill reality became frayed...

We played major league and we parlayed in minor
scales...
Until reality became frayed and frail
The scenario shifts but the sounds never fade nor
fail....
The scenario shifts but the sounds never fade...

Even the silences betray a secret ... far sweeter
scerenade...
As we sailed on a sea of natural endomorphines
That urged us to Engage....
We Plaaayed ! But only played......

Getting lost in your own subtext
As you strain to slip into something
Ever-so-slightly more subversive.
If talk were text you'd speak in cursive.

And at best what serendipity with which
You've been blessed to have and possess.
An unpredictable irresponsibility
That becomes the ultimate test.

Voracious and as vixen-like as ever... In your
vexation
You villify as you virulently voice your views.
Knocking spots off Emelda-Marcos
As you gather up your Oceans of shoes...
Still there's a Blues both Sea and Sky doth share
Subjected to Sunshine's Omniscient glare
And as you appeared to glow
You were Eclipsed
Nay ! Sheltered by the shadow
Of the bimbo-limbo dancer Who'd come and go
Jangling... Nay ! Babbling
About Umm Kalthoum and Pablo Picasso
Or was it Groucho Marx and Freda Carlo

Bluesology.

The Blues is a school / And a down home place.
Where folks freely discuss / What they feels taking place.
From the darkness a treasure / Only hearts can measure.
The Soul deeper it gets, Blues-folks like it better.

This Blues is a college / Built on poor folks knowledge
Where you follow the trees / To the heart of the forest.
Pray for justice and truth /Speak with clowns and fools.
Keep your heart as your proof, and you'll always be cool.

This is a Bluesology... And I 'm a scholar of the Blues .
I graduated in Nothin' ! Nothin ' left to loose !

In the Blues University / Wisdom comes from adversity.
Taste the turmoil and strife / Pepper spice of your life.
Add some toil and struggle / And the flavour is doubled
Soulfood's on the menu, once you burst that bubble.

You can only arrive / At a sense of yourself

By confronting your fears / And through nobody else.

Ugliness comes from fear / You can take it or leave it.

The gifts of Love's tears, is Nature's way to relieve it.

This is a Bluesology... And I 'm a scholar of the Blues .

I graduated in Nothin' ! Nothin ' left to loose !

Threads.

In the dead of the stillness...
In the still of the night...

When the sharpest eye
could barely discern
a piece of black thread
from
a piece of white...

There in lies Love's most hidden meanin'...

The resolution
of all the meanin's
to all a the answers
to all a the empty squares...
filled with all of the words
from all of the crossword puzzles of the Ancient World...

No matter what the time...

The radiance of human virtue shine... with
an ominous light...

Especially in the dread of the stillness of the still of
dhe night ! La Shay !

La Shay was a secret treasure
Hidden within the Void
Dwelling within the moment
With nothing to avoid
No name was there nor attributes
No image form or place
All that we know has passed away
Except the yearning for His grace

And I am The One Whom I Know that I am
La Shay ! I am Nothing ! I am Only a Man !

Glory be to the One
That none can describe
Who abides in the Stillness
Where the Unseen hides
Before the first sound
Formed a single dot
Nothing was written
Not even a jot
Nothing was with Him
But His Self alone
In an ocean of Mercy
That desired to be known

And I am The One Whom I Know that I am
La Shay ! I am Nothing ! I am Only a Man !

Material Lovers.

The starless shadow of a stark sales pitch
stagnates.
Silhouetted against the surly sales- assistant's
striped shirt.

Stratified city dwellers stand guard
Both sides of a demarcation zone.
Sterile starlets startled by instant success
Man the counter's

Consumers of lonely encounters
Via the virtual telephone.
Roam aimlessly from store to store.

As silent citizens seep out of control
Drool over shop-soiled catalogue gear.
Second hand trade secrets to wear and share.

Across the counter an odd pair.
Selling free samples of fresh air.
Ex-vending machine sachets.

Water in this desert of human compassion.
Where intelligence is artificial, drug induced
Or just rationed 'til it's out of fashion.

The wild raucous noise of wanton wishes.
Rebellious rivalries and ribald revelries.

Raunchy serotonin levels heavily dishevelled.
Modern mating rituals leaving a musty mildew

On the minds of the manipulators of meaning.

Who swell with pride at the killing streets.
Of Wilderness city.
The non-comitant non-entity.

Treasure.

It's hard to explain this age old treasure
No Nubian rubies, emeralds or pearls
Antiques of a quality noone can measure
Pure silver and gold from another world

Evolved at the source of the River Nile
Flowering slower than Human patience.
As esoteric as a hidden smile
As revolutionary as the Ancients.

Serenity Hmmm...
Serenity Yeay! Yeah!

Source of life and human will
The stuff that makes the Earth go round
Ideas impossible to kill
Escape the sound of verbs and nouns.

Human existance a fragile freedom
Saved but for a second, then thrown and lost.
No one remembers original names
Life's lamentations count the cost.
Caught up in the endless game
Truth stands alone amidst the dross.

Serenity Hmmm...

Serenity Yeay! Yeah!

Focus in on Nothing
Meditate on Empty space
Sweet none existence
Our place in The Placeless Place.
Nothing can exist without Nothing
Womb of the formless night
Any journey worth it's plotting
Must traverse the Sea of Black Light.

Luminous splendour of Emptiness
The Void we can't resist...
The All Abiding Consciousness.
The Presence that isn't quite there.
The Majesty Unmanifest...
Surrounds us everywhere.

Serenity Hmmm...
Serenity Yeay! Yeah!

Knowledge belongs to Believers
Worldlyness to achievers.
Some seek pleasure / Some seek leisure
Some search for that hidden Treasure
Riches only Hearts can measure.

Serenity Hmmm...
Serenity Yeay! Yeah!

Venus in Transit.

Venus is the planet of love

To the Children of the Earth
Sulphuric acid hangs in clouds
Above this globe of many hearths
Volcanic activity populates
It's hectic surface
Still our hearts as pure as doves
Are drawn towards it's purpose.

Venus in Transit

Essentially we long to taste
The hot kiss of your fiery face
Even though we know we'd just dissolve
It never weakens our resolve
To merge like moths within the flame
No thought of infamy or fame
No thought of pleasure, Peace, nor Pain

Venus in Transit

The yearning to become as One
The Moon that cancels out my Sun
Instinctive leap towards the heat
No wings nor feet just hearts that beat
With Remembrance of the Holy Name
That takes the Soul back home again.
What's named is constant and remains
Beyond all naming and all names.

Water.

Where the crystal waters flow
fresh thoughts usher forth

from the thinness of the air
take root in the Earth and grow.

The Way is of Water no illusion
Sweet and as precious as the greenness
That sparkles with the shimmering freshness of
spring
And Love is a melody that floats on the wind
As gently as the sound of a butterfly's wing

Amidst the fruitful pastures of unseen dreams
The Verdiant / The Natural / The Tranquil / The
Serene...
Clear is the river that began as a trickle
And grew into a raging stream.
Each waterfall a cascading dream

Silver rapids feed lakes of tranquility
Water itself becoming a living entity
Fresh, this font of inspirational profusion
Gushing in torrents of abundance
Running with the wind
Drinking in the rain, a line, a wave, a cloud again.

This way of water it's movement is moon light
It's secret a precious gem
An amorous pearl encased in the shell
Of the solitary Love of The Beloved

Remembrances waiting to be freed
Oceans of eternity to vast to know
A tidal wave to wash us free of Human need
That carries us along in it's generous flow

And this Love is a melody that floats on the wind
As light as the sound of a butterfly's wing

Cleansing from the roots of The Beloved's Creation
Water springing from the rocks of purification
This is the reality of Light's variations
Where the crystal waters flow
Green shoots usher forth
Verdiant pastures of the serene
Fresh green thoughts from the tranquil, the unseen.

For His are all the forests woodlands
Hillsides, valleys, meadows and fields
Fruit ripe on the bough-Harvests in full yield
And life is as precious as the water that sparkles
With the shimmering freshness of spring
And your Love is a melody
That floats on the wind
As natural
As the sound of a butterfly's wing.

Celebrate!

Yeah ! Yea-yah !
Jamming the way of the Believer
In a Dervish manner
I've got Blues etiquette
And English grammar.

So let the rap ring out
Like a Blacksmith's hammer

In a style that could use
A little Jazz piannah.

It's in the nature
Of my natural-born
Mersey-side roots
Allah tempers my nature
My Soul bares fruit

Knowledge of self understanding
And timeless truth.
My Shiekh moved with the beat
Of the street as his proof.

So if the Spirit Moves yah and yah feel to relate
Make a joyful noise and lets celebrate
Make a joyful noise and lets celebrate.
I said Lets celebrate Yeah-Yeah ! Yeah-yeah !

A daily ritual ! Prayer !
You could call it habitual
I call it merely doing
What comes natural...
Celebrating life whirling
Sometimes like a Dervish
Poor folks dancing with remembrance
So consider it a service.

Sufi-Blues-Gospel-News
Soulful truth of our youth
Pumping bass-lines in the basement
Singing love-songs on the roof Yeah !

Spiritual at conception

Like the power of the sun
Mystic love that links creation
Where the inspiration comes from
Some call it The Presence
Second Only to None
I like to call it Al Wahid
The One & Only One

So if the Spirit Moves yah and yah feel to relate
Make a joyful noise and lets celebrate
Make a joyful noise and lets celebrate.
I said Lets celebrate Yeah-Yeah ! Yeah-yeah !

As recited by the throngs
That sang the Gospel songs
Inspired by the Freedom
For which they longed
Gives a whole new meaning
To the word forgiving
Thru blood stained seasons
New reasons for living

Wounded hearts left bleeding
Through open minds
Finding the Oneness of all People
At the Dawn of Time

Rising above it as Brothers and sisters
Together ! And together !
And together ! We shine!

We Shine ! We shine ! We Be Shine !
Together ! And together !

And together ! We shine!

So if the Spirit Moves yah and yah feel to relate
Make a joyful noise and lets celebrate
Make a joyful noise and lets celebrate.
I said Lets celebrate Yeah-Yeah ! Yeah-yeah !
Lets celebrate Ah-ah ! Ah-ah !

1'001 Nights.

North of The Sahara or just North of the Watford
Gap

Cosmopolitan people in a post millenium melting
pot

In a white hot inner city night spot

Everybody get flat when you hear the gun shot.

Others don't stop they just keep on Boppin' like
their having some fun

One or two students start dropping off one by one.

All that glitters is sold as gold on a rope.

Fortunes are made, others are told as hope.

Another Western Life-style Pop flirtation

With a groovy ethnocentric orientation.

They said...

"Flavour of the month, get it down on plastic.

Yeah ! That's kicking. OK Fantastic!"

100'1 Nights of static in the attic. Getting hyped on static in the attic... Aah Yeah!

Hold on tight cos were going on a trip

That was The Lounge-Core DJ in the day-glow strip

And with a flip and a dip and a skip the cat took off

Reached a peak tried to speak

Then he just chewed his own lid of.

Mass hallucination is like a media malady.

Public opinion another marketing strategy.

Plumb jam body slam, it's the latest thing.

Values diluted in a dizzy dope mix down.

Superficial prejudices

Prey on something like you lower senses

Evolution cash flow commodity expenses

Merchandised lifestyles and disposable realities

Ane these are the vanities were sold as niceties.

(And I thought they wouldn't like that but...

They said...

"Flavour of the month, get it down on plastic.

Yeah ! That's kicking. OK Fantastic!"

100'1 Nights of static in the attic. Getting hyped on static in the attic... Aah Yeah!

Paris to Peking - Beijng to Baghdad

Everybody trippin' and flippin' and drippin" over the latest fad.

You buy a style designered good style, and in a while

You get bitten somewhere sinful by the style crocodile.

Smiling faces strobe lights and a wacky Rap attack.

Be nice to the Management lads. No smack! No crack!

Refugees from The Wirral Peninsula hard at work

The Midnight Express is stressed and kinda outa beserk.

Extras from the set of Baron Munshhausen.

Out to lunch no regrets. What's happening!

Temptation's set back just watching the game.

The Reservation did an Indian dance that could

bring on the rain.

They said...

"Flavour of the month, get it down on plastic.

Yeah ! That's kicking. OK Fantastic!"

100'1 Nights of static in the attic. Getting hyped on static in the attic..

Aah Yeah!

In a corner of the House a little groups stands out

You know that these guys are serious, I mean this was never in doubt.

The leader's face wore a look of distaste

As if defending somethin' similar to a personal headspace.

Someone casts a complacent glance

Reveals an attitude towards chance. In tones that convey alternative intentions...

Not a lot.. but just enough... Just enough to mention.

Eyes clocking the time I move in. I unwind.

It's like African Dance culture has surfaced World wide.

I feel as Black people we taught the Wild West, how

to socialise.

I know that's not a bad idea, but I wonder was it wise.

They said...

"Flavour of the month, get it down on plastic.

Yeah ! That's kicking. OK Fantastic!"

100'1 Nights of static in the attic. Getting hyped on static in the attic... Aah Yeah!

Couldn't trust what I'd seen or heard.

Double standards perceptions blurred.

I reached for my guide to the Unknown Universe.

My pocket book of Sufi Rap Prayers.

I quoted 'Roses from the Heart', text and verse.

Line 1, section 2, paragraph 3...

What difference does it make to you

About what it all means to me?

When the hot sun shines... Shines!

It refreshes my face, my body, my taste, my mind.

Light is a Universal focal point of Equilibrium.

Applicable to All people. Any space time continuum.

Chapter 3, paragraph 2, subheading 1, On What to do?

Whats going on? And what does it all mean to you...

Do not pass go! Do not collect 200 get hip!

Don't trade your mind for a metaphor on plastic that's sick.

Don't space out on the squares in that jazzy check jacket.

Don't let mind dissolve into a Souless racket

Don't loose your wits involved with a perspex packet...

Just dance like a Dervish till Life's rhythm is mastered.

They said...

"Flavour of the month, get it down on plastic.

Yeah ! That's kicking. OK Fantastic!"

100'1 Nights of static in the attic. Getting hyped on static in the attic. Aah Yeah! And it's like that...

Jape.

Sumtimes I think dhat deh best Preacher
is deh stand-uP comic.......

But dhen again won has tuh consider context
which brings us around to acumen
Political and social
cultural and notional
a joke or a Poem
dePending on dhe PeoPle
ids always quite oPtional
I Mean.... Peter PiPer Picked a Peck uf
Pickled PePPer Corn ... Didn't he ?
He did ? Didn't he... Please tell me he did!
I mean dhats wot I woz always brought uP to
believe.......

Birth of a Legendary Poem.

I have series of leitmotifs that codify the struggle
of my particular section of the Black Diasporan
Community's, struggle

against Racism historically, and currently. Slavery
is one of them.

And as it has turned out, one of the main ones.
Why ? Well...

If there's one poem that I'm known for. One poem
that stands out above the rest in my 40 years as an
internationally touring, performance poet, it's the
poem Slavepool.

It's a poem that started about 40 years ago, a poem
that took me twenty years to finish. It only really

completed itself during the Millennium Year.

You'll see why, you'll also see that there is a subtle irony in the how, and the why of it.

The history of the poem Slavepool illustrates how, over time my personal drive towards freedom of expression as an artist, has overlapped into, and in many instances become recognised as the freeing of an aspect of my 'Communities' voice.

The poem has a developed a history, that is interwoven with the history of the Community it speaks on behalf of, by the extent to which it has carried the voice of that 'Community' from which it was born, into the main stream, in a way that has never before been achieved.

40 years on the Poem has developed a life all unto itself.

It's a story that is reflected in, the history of the poem itself.

It's a story that I will begin for you, not long after the opening of the Albert Dock as Liverpool's new tourist attraction.

One mid-Summer, Saturday afternoon, Levi Tafari, John Maglone, both fellow members of The Ministry of Love, and myself, had been hired by The Albert Dock Festival people to perform around the dock as wandering players. Cool! What's not to like?

We'd turn up at a contractually agreed site-location, and one of us would get a groove going on the congas, while the other one recited a poem over the beat. Then we'd swap, and the other person'd play while his partner played conga. Then we'd move on to a new location around The Dock.

It went well people were digging our act. We set up outside the Merseyside Maritime Museum, next to the big shiny-black anchor, doing our thing, and it started to rain.

So I says "OK, lets moved into the foyer everybody else has, it's warm, dry and there's a big crowd in there sheltering from the rain, we can do a set for them." So we did.

I got a rhythm going on congas Levi did the 'Conservative Blues' rap, as this was during the post-80's uprising, mid-Thatcher Era. It went down well. The crowd of mostly tourists, loved it.

But I could see that the doorman's neck had been slightly put out. Next thing Levi played congas, and I performed the Talking Blues-poem 'Slavepool', and before we knew it, we were out on our necks.

It could have been Levi's dodgy conga playing, but I don't think it was. It was the poem 'Slavepool'.

When confronted with the question the question "Why?" the angry, and somewhat indignant doorman had replied, "Liverpool never made it's wealth from Slavery. It made it's money from sugar, tobacco, and cotton !" .

I asked him who had picked the cotton, and cut the sugar cane, worked the tobacco plantations, but he got all redneck on me.

So I left it at that. We went to the office got our wages, and left.

The irony is, that when the museum had opened, the Black presence in Liverpool had been on the museums agenda, and I'd been invited to take part in a panel of guest speakers, alongside Peter Fryer, the author of 'Staying Power' the definitive history of the Black presence in the UK from pre-Roman times up until the post-Colonial era, at the time anyway, and also people like 'Kemetic Educational Guidance', a Manchester based Afro-Centric group of creative scholars.

And of course I had to recite the poem. It was a great honour for me, and the poem. The Community was there in the form of Liverpool Anti-Racist Community Arts, directed by Ibrahim Thompson. Truth was being recognised. Never the less, for several years after that, I told the story of the 'Doorman', everytime I performed the poem, in schools, theatres, on radio and TV, and in interviews with the press, throughout the UK, USA, and Europe.

The irony emerged in greater detail when the Merseyside Maritime Museum, decided to open up a Trans-Atlantic Slavery Gallery, as a direct result of my recital of that infamous poem.

It became a controversial issue with some of the Black Community, as par for the course. A bully got in my face aggressively telling me, "I should have wrote that!" I replied, "What you mean is that wish you'd have wrote it. Jealousy had reared it's ugly vicious head.

The museum's Community liaison worker got scapegoated, as flack-catchers usually do, that was followed the death threats, and all the usual business.

BBC Radio Four's Black current affairs programme, 'In Living Colour' were set to broadcast a live debate from The maritime Museum, the panel was made up of various spokes-people from the Community, PhD's, people working in education and stuff, and the museum staff, and defenders. I was commissioned by the BBC to write a poem for the event, based on some notes they'd sent me from Seventeenth century documents concerning the reality of Slavery in Liverpool. Everyone wanted to be seen to be apart of this historic awakening.

I did a poem called 'Salt in the Wound', that rested on the side of the Community. Personally I was sick of the subject of Slavery by then, and the poem Slavepool. But the poem was destined to live on, and a demand grew for it that was greater than any other poem I'd ever done on the subject of Slavery.

Next thing I know, the Museum's Community Liaison Office contacted me, because they wanted to make the poem, the basis of an outreach project they had been planning for schools, something Levi and myself had been doing already as Community Artists, in collaboration with Liverpool City Council's Art's and Cultural Industries Unit, and North West Arts.

Never the less their request was most satisfying.

They called on me to give talks, and recite several times after that, and at various official occasions, and related events. The poem was about seven years old at this point, but it wasn't the first time it had tasted recognition. It had first appeared in a film in 1981, by a Scandinavian TV Company, about Liverpool's post-Riot situation, and the Militant era, complete with scenes of Granby Street, South African style policing, riot vans, and alsation dogs.

In the film I was interviewed at home, and then I read Slavepool, in an early prose form, much different than it is today. For dramatic effect I read it in the cemetery of The Anglican Cathedral, with my Foster daughter Tanya Khalifa next to me.

I pointed out the cemetery of the Liverpool
Anglican Cathedral, so I could point out the names
of Sea Captains, and merchants on the graves.
People who had died in places like Barbados,
and Georgia, all plantation owners. I linked the
graves with the original owners of the magnificent
architectural achievements, that still exist in
abundance throughout the South end of the
City, despite the rash demolitions of uncultured,
myopic Sixties town planners.

I talked about the irony of these Georgian terraces
now being the habitation of Blacks, Bohemians,
and students.

I recited the poem for UK TV around 1983, to
Dawn French during an interview for the Channel
Four programme 'Swanks'. In fact I recited the
poem on radio, TV, and in the media so often
throughout the Eighties, that I got wel and truly
chokka with it.

Each time I'd recite it, I'd tell myself I'm dropping
this poem. And each time I'd bin it, I'd receive
a letter, or a phone-call requesting for it, to be
published in some anthology or other, or used in
some way or other on radio, or TV.

For example, around 1985, the lines

"Four Hundred Years of Shackles and Chains"
was taken from the third verse... And used as
the title of a study of Racism in The Arts on

Merseyside, conducted by Liverpool City Council and Merseyside Arts.

It also became the title for, and was recited in an educational film sponsored by, the Liverpool City Council, and North West Arts concerning the history of Liverpool's Black Community, as the oldest Black community in Europe, put together in

'The Charles Wooten Centre a local Black Education Centre', named after Charles Wooten the first Blackman to die in the anti-Black pogroms of Liverpool's dark past.

It was used as the opening page of a bibliography, listing all the existing books on the Slavery, 'The Black Presence in Liverpool', a small reference book published by The Liverpool City Council's Libraries and Leisure Dept, for which I wrote the introduction.

It appeared in BBC Radio 2's Music Machine, for whom I researched an half hour educational programme on 'Rap and the Roots of the Oral Tradition In Ancestral Religious Practises', and 'Tribal Systems of Education', around about 1988. It had moved people during the service, the Women's Gospel Choir had been reduced to tears, various people, even grown men had wept.

An extremely emotive, live performance appeared as a full broadcast,on BBC Radio 2 this time, as part of a Multi-Faith Service held in The Liverpool

Anglican Cathedral for the Souls of the Slaves who'd died during the Middle Passage. It also went out as part of a news report, covering that event for Radio 5. The reporter hadn't caught the actual performance during the service on tape, so after the service the BBC 5, cub-reporter had me trying to capture the passionate-delivery, with which he thought I'd performed it as part of the actual service, but of course such rituals can't be reconstructed cold for the camera or the mic.

Afterwards millionaire Peter Moor came up to me, and congratulated me, as did everybody as usual. I even received a card from Peter Moor further expressing his appreciation, and suggesting that I call the poem, 'Slaverpool'. I rejected his idea. He may be the millionaire, but I'm the poet.

The Multi-Faith Service was about 1989, the poem was like a son to me by now. I was proud of him. Who would let a stranger rename their child. It was first published by The Windows Project, around 1983, in a short collection of my work entitled 'Da-Da Drum', and has since been published in two other collections.

The first being "In Context", a 1991 publication that was part of the 'Jazz Writer in Context', Educational Project aimed at Schools, in and around the North West sponsored again by Liverpool City Council's Arts and Cultural Industries Unit, and

North West Arts Literature Development Office, headed by Theresa Griffin, now a local Labour candidate.

The second a pamphlet entitled 'Hip-Hop Sulook', four poems that summarise the inner-journey of my Rap years. The poem has been recorded many times, in many forms, with many different sets of musicians, and DJ's over the years, for radio and TV, and for touring shows.

It has mutated into many forms to fit the many collaborations, from avante garde Jazz, Afro-Jazz, Free-Jazz, Funk, Blues, Hip-hop, Reggae to even a Rocky-Soul version that was recorded for Radio Merseyside around 1986, with a band called The Ministry of Love.

that sounded like a cross between Gil Scot-Heron and Jimi Hendrix.

In 1996 it was recorded for a Radio Merseyside live hook-up with New York slam poets, the Vibe Chameleons. It was also recorded on Radio Merseyside, when I took part in a summary of ten years of the Liverpool Music Scene, that ran from midnight to four am,

New Years eve 1990, two listeners phoned in record requests for me.

One requested Eric B and Rakim's 'You got Soul', and the other listener requested Public Enemy's,

'Rebel without a Pause'. That's how I entered the Nineties.

I thought I've gotta lay this poem to rest once and for all. Ten years, is old for a poem. But history hadn't finished with it yet.

As a solo poem, or accompanied by a gig review, or an interview, the poem has appeared in poetry collections, and writing anthologies, arts magazines, and educational journals throughout the UK, Europe, and parts of the USA right through the Nineties.

The fact that the poem is on several websites, as text and as a soundbyte, in places like The Wordhoard website from out of Huddersfield, and Muhammad Yusef's 'Blues and Rebellion' site from out of Birmingham, means it is actually out there on it's own now. Fending for itself. It's a poem come of age that fled the nest.

In between 1997-99, I performed twice in New York, and twice in The Caribbean. I performed the poem, when I came a joint second in the Poetry Slam, at The Nuyorican Poetry Café, Manhattan, New York's Lower East Side, and home of the Poetry Slam phenomenon.

The performance went out on national TV, as part of 'New York is Book Country'.

I also did radio in the states, the previous year, and

performed it on TV, and radio in The Caribbean as part of Carnival week.

I performed it when I hosted the opening dinner entertainment's at 'The Collegium of African American Research' conference, in the Adelphi Hotel Liverpool, where I met many top scholars of African-American history from around The World, amongst them Henry Louis Gates Jr, one of the foremost in his field, someone I'd read a lot of during my MA. As a consequence of that performance a copy was requested by the English Departments, of Pace University New York, New York State University, The Shonberg Museum and Archives of African American History in Harlem, and a copy shares the honoured position of being one of three poems framed, and hanging on the wall of the Head of African American Studies in The University of Laguna, Canary Isles.

The recital of Slavepool the poem, was the one of main ingredients in a film produced by a very creative film maker, and sincere Human being of Irish descent, called Wayne O'brien from Warrington.

Wayne made a film about the relationship of the legacy of

Slavery, and Black art in Liverpool today, as part of his MA in Film Making, at Warrington University.

The title of the film originally was to be 'Slavepool',

after the poem, which played a major part in the film, but it was later changed to 'Loosen the Shackles'. The film was put to Channel Four, who loved it, and it was screened twice as part of their 'Art For Art Sakes' series, August 2000. The Community loved it, from crack-heads off the street, to Gran-Muthas.

I was truly humbled, not just by this but by the response of the people in the City, in general. All races, all sections loved it, and let me know.

What was funny was the fact that people who I know had heard it dozens of time over the years, people who I'd clocked at lots of recitals in the past, swore that they'd only heard it for the first time, once they'd seen it on TV. That showed me a great deal, about people and poetry. The film went on to win several film awards, and even now is used as a model in film making courses, throughout the UK.

The Merseyside Maritime Museum continued heap irony upon irony, as they launched the 'Annual Slavery Memorial' event, that calls for the establishment of an Eternal Flame type of monument,

to be ignited in memory of the victims of 'The Trans-Atlantic Slave Trade'. An idea originated, and initiated by the now deceased Labour MP, the late-great Bernie Grant in 1999, and carried forward after his death, by his wife Sharon in the following Millennium Year.

By which time I'd become the City's official Slavery Poet, and as such I was invited to recite 'Slavepool' at the Memorial Service.

In the Anglican Cathedral rubbing shoulders with such distinguished guests as Sharon Grant, The Lord Mayor of Liverpool, who probably knows the poem better that me by now, and Professor Fred Hinckley, head of Psychiatry at Birmingham University, and somebody whose essay I had published twenty years previous in a Rasta magazine,

that I used to edit and contribute to around 1980, called the 'I-Conception'.

It had grown from marginalised, dissident voice to people's poet.

It was a Mandela of a poem. As much as I was bored with it. I had to give it respect. It kept going. Summer 1999 the poem 'Slavepool'

was instrumental in an interview, and group discussion I had with Melvin Bragg, concerning the linguistic specifics of a Black Scouse vernacular form of oral expression. Parts of which were recorded as part of the BBC series "The Routes of English", an eighteen part radio series on a Thousand Years of Spoken English, accompanied by a set of three books, and six CD's.

The poem was becoming indelibly carved into the history of Liverpool's Black Community, as Melvin talked about Slavery, Black poetry, and Liverpool. People all over the country were phoning me to say that they'd heard it.

By the advent of Y2K, the poem had become the basis for an article I was requested to write for the Lord Mayors Millennium report, on the future of Liverpool, entitled 'Scouser 2000/ A Poet's View'.

Following this as if in it's wake, came the Liverpool City Council's Official Recognition of The City's Role in The Trans-Atlantic Slavetrade. A cosmetic affair with imported African libation experts from Manchester, to lay to rest the ghosts of any African Slaves

that may be still lingering around The Pier Head.

An imported congregation of Black Gospelites from Bristol, a Sister-Slave-port with Liverpool undergoing similar healing rituals. My role was to recite 'Slavepool' in St Nicholas's Church down by the river. The honoured guests were some clergy from Richmond Virginia, and the Black deputy Mayor of Richmond. Richmond being the gateway to Slavery in North America, and as such a US equivalent to Liverpool.

African Ju-Ju Chiefs, an ancestral King maker from Ghana, and various local activists, established elders from the Black Community …

Those responsible for petitioning The City, for recognition of Africa's contribution to it's Actual physical establishment, and it's prosperous past.

I recited Surah Balad, The Chapter of The City, from the Holy Koraan, in English, and Arabic. "It starts with I swear by this city".

Then it goes on to suggest that one of the ways of tackling the steep ascent of overcoming Mankind's imperfections of greed, and cruelty is to "Free a slave." It fitted perfectly.

The clergy loved it, the American Priest like many original old school Dreads like Brother Bob told me he had a Koran and that he was going to read it again when he got home, as I'd shown him it in a light he hadn't seen it in before.

Then I gave a talk on the survival of African Spirituality... During Slavery via the oral tradition of the Muslim Slaves.

I mentioned pre-Slavery Islam in the Americas the Mission of Mansa Musa, 800 years prior to Columbus. I spoke of The Sunnah's revival during the ministry of Al Haj Malik Shabbaz, Malcolm X.

And I pulled together Dreader-Dread quotes from

The Tradition that Malcolm became famous for reviving

Amongst African-Americans, quotes like ...

"Educate a man and you Liberate him. Educate a woman and you Liberate the Nation."

And, "Knowledge is the lost property of the Believer where ever he may find it",

And, "Seek knowledge even if you have to travel to China, for there is reputed to be Wisdom there",.

And, "It is incumbent on every Beliving man and woman to seek Knowledge",

And, "Those who leave home in search of knowledge truly are Believers".

To bring it all on home locally, I tied it all up by mentioning my personal chain of transmission from Al Haj Malik Al-Shabbazz, through the late-great, Sheikh Sulieman Al Hadi of the Masjid al Taqwa, Brooklyn,

New York, the spiritual force behind 'The Last Poets'.

I spoke of his disciple Jalal Mansur Nurridin, also from New York.

Resident in Toxteth for the last ten years or so, keeping the oral tradition alive amongst seekers of knowledge locally.

I dedicated a Rasta-Gospel poem, called "Hope "to the our Black Gospel guests in a Motown styley.

They seemed not to be impressed, I got the

distinct impression that they thought that I was patronising them, but that wasn't my intention. I'd also playfully chided the African Ju-Ju people

for bringing witch-craft into the Church? And they'd laughed so I was just entering into the spirit of mutual tolerance.

It was a beautiful sharing.

Some of the Afro-centric, secular section of the Black community, showed anti-Islamic signs, but they all had to acknowledge Malcolm,

and The Last Poets who are Universally loved throughout the Black World, and beyond.

The new version of Slavepool emerged from retirement, as part of the

Liverpool University's 'Africa Two Thousand Conference'.

A week long affair that brought together scholars of

Black and African related subjects from around he World.

I was invited by Dr Mark Christian local member of the Black Community, now teaching in the States, to contribute the poem Slavepool as an introduction to a talk being given by Professor Abdul Hakim Quick, of Capetown, via Toronto-

Canada, the USA, and Kingston-Jamaica. Professor Quick is the author of the book 'Deeper Roots', and an invaluable source of information on the history of Islam in Africa, and throughout The Americas, pre-Slavery and post-Slavery.

His talk was supported by the multi-media computor aided skills, of Sidi Muhammad Shariff of the Oakland Ghetto, California, USA, Who has studied Black African History insuch places as Mauritania, Nigeria, Syria, and Sudan.

After the recital and the talk Professor Ali Mazrui, from the States via Kenya, via the UK who wrote the ten part Channel Four Series entitled "The Africans", now teaching in a University in the America came up to me and just said, "Thank You for the poem". I was elated and humbled at the same time. Professor Mazrui, also asked for a copy of the poem, as did Professor Dorothy Badejo, another American expert on West African history and culture. I gave them both a copy of my self-published slim volume, "In Context".

I would never have imagined, the poem 'Slavepool' has become engraved into the history of not only, both the Community and the City... But established academics and institutions across the Globe.

Due partly by being an active part of the process of bringing about mainstream awareness of the voice of the marginalised.

Which is nothing more than the process of democracy in theory.

What was once perceived of as a threatening underground,

dissident perspective has been absorbed into the official story.

And so much so that Liverpool's role in the Trans-Atlantic Slave Trade, and it's position as Europe's oldest Black Community have placed it high up on the slavery Pilgrimage Trail, that takes in Africa, The Americas, and The Caribbean.

All of a sudden The City's aware that it's Black history could be a major pull for rich African-Americans, and researchers in Black history in general, World-wide. So just when I was thinking that twenty years is far too long to be reciting the same poem, I'm already a year into the New Millennium, and the demand has increased.

Due to the renewed interest at governmental levels

regarding issues of Citizenship, Identity, Global awareness, and sustainable development, not to mention increasing racism towards asylum seekers.

I could go on but there is no point as I couldn't keep track of how much its been used and downloaded due to the new tech-knowledgy.

I Googled Slavepool once ... and discovered that the poem is plastered all over the Internet. In various forms

And recieves regular listens downloads, and likes via Mix FM, Soundcloud, Youtube.

I Googled my name once and it came up next to the poem

In so many diverse contexts.

As the hookline says; "Things'll never be the same"...

Jam to Celebrate 40 Years of Roger Hill's 'Popular Music Show' (PMS) for Radio Merseyside. 1977-2017.

1977 two sevens clash. Culture bash.
God Save The Queen. Toasting live with
Jah Crasher's DJ's on Radio Merseyside
Jubilee Year in Ite's Gold and Green
Caught on tape for posterity's sake
A moment of Merseyside's Popular music scene.

Mohawks on Mathew Street
Dreadlocks in the Blues Dance
Studded leather jackets
Peroxide blonde quiffs

Combat fatigues and Dr Martins
Heavey Dread Dub Trance
Steel pulse and the Slits
Rasta Punk Romance
It's the Zeitgeist so it just fits.

Pets collars for chokers
Tarnished nail varnish
Mega dramatic make up
Uni Sex Ganja smokers
In various designs
Safety pin piercings
A sign of the times.

Probe Records The Armadillo
Blood & Lip Stick in
Aunt Twacky's Bazaar
Rock Against Racism
Charabang to London
Hackney Victoria Park.

Anti Nazi League Silly Billies
Heard the Clash playing
Police and Thieves...

Stewart Copeland's crisp drumming
Funkadelic's Presence of a Brain
Gospel Blues Spiritual Humming
Watching Stanley Clarke play
School Days live @ Eric's.
LiverpoolSchool of Language, Dream & Pun.

Army & Navy store's gear
Seditionaries bondage wear...

Geek Chique Elvis & Costello
All Retro-Rehashed with a dash of kitsch
To raise the pitch...
Like Joyce in his tower Morello.

Improvised images to readily wear
Anarchy in the UK clothes industry
Cut price fashion A slash, a rip, or a tear.

Rock & Roll reinvented by the Pistols
The Buzzcocks, Damned and the Jam
Reggae Culture and Inner City dispair
Drawing on creativity from
No where and everywhere.

A whole generation learning fast.
The over indulgence of the under-class.
New Wave bravely playing it's part
An explosion of popular culture
In fashion, music, dance, and art.

From The Sun at Night to Visual Stress
Earthbeat clubland to Larks in the Parks
DJ's blurring generic boundries with
Beat box sonic foundries.
Creating memories witin the heart.

Brown Girls in 2-Tone X Ray specs
And Black and White checks
At Punky-Reggae-Ska parties
Scallywags & Arty Farties.

Proto-type Hip-Hop's Cosmic Jazz
Rewiring and transforming the record decks
For scratching digital hyroglyphics
Into sacred vinyl creating new sounds
Of rhythmic excitement, and non-specifics.
Sound systems test the decibel limits.

There I am with the Mighty Wah !
Headlining above Aswad. Wow !
The People's Festival St George's Plateau.
The Story of the Blues. Top of the charts.

Now it's a midnite to 4am session
New Year 1990 Radio Merseyside
Hanover Street next to the Friends Meting House
Live broacast with Roger Hill
Lots of members of local bands are presesnt
Summarizing the past decade of 80's music
On Merseyside. A moment of pride
when two records are requested for me
By anonymous members of the public.
Eric B & Rakim's "You Got Soul"
and Public Enemy No1's
"Rebel Without a Pause".
That was better than any applause.

We shared non stop stories, anecdotes, and music,
Non-stop talk. We say how we walk.

We look back over 40 years of the Popuar Music
show
Eclectic, experimental, innovative, and so
necessary
Allowing us artists & musicians exposure, and
access
To a bigger world that we shared with the nation,
The World of the Visionary.

Over those many many years. PMS channeling all
of the Culture that people were sharing...
All that energy, the Energy of all those dreams, and
ideas,
Schemes, themes and reems of creativity and...
Some sprouting to full blossom. Others gone but
not forgotten.

Translated into music and song,
A vibration held in focus by the broad, and
conscious vision... of DJ Roger Hill. From 1977 to
2017 and all the years
Of sonic exploration and cultural research in
between.

PMS and the Merseyside popular music scene
A pool of life, a veritable sea of dreams.

Printed in Great Britain
by Amazon